Your Inner State
Is Your Fate

By Kedarji

I0616271

The Bhakta School of Transformation, Inc.
Youngstown, Ohio

Your Inner State
Is Your Fate

By Kedarji

Copies of this book may be ordered through booksellers or by contacting:

The Bhakta School of Transformation, Inc.
330-623-7388 Ext 10

NityanandaShaktipatYoga.org

ISBN: 979-8-218-60550-6

Printed in the United States of America

Contents

Introduction

This book is for those who are newcomers to Nityananda Shaktipat Yoga. It is also written for those who want to renew their daily spiritual practice with a beginner's mind. Also, in this book I use the words "Sadguru," "Siddha Guru," "Shaktipat Siddha Guru," "Shaktipat Sadguru," and "Guru" interchangeably. They are the same reference to a Shaktipat Guru who is a spiritual leader.

"The Heart is the hub of all sacred places. Go there and roam."
~Bhagawan Nityananda of Ganeshpuri

This world is a pleasure garden to roam in with unconditional love, total peace and complete joy. It is not meant as a source of anxiety, frustration, fear, jealousy, greed, anger, delusion, and conditionality. Anxiety, frustration, fear, jealousy, greed, anger, delusion, and conditionality – these are of the mind only. Once the restlessness and dross of the mind is removed the heart is revealed in all its purity, love and light.

Your inner state is your fate. It is how your life is created. Your inner state determines what you will experience and how you will experience it. It determines your life lessons and how easy or difficult those lessons will be. It regulates the number of impressions that are created in your subtle body, impressions that not only dictate the course of your life but how many more lifetimes you will have to lead before you become one with your inner Self, how many more lifetimes you will have to lead before you attain the happiness and freedom that is your birthright.

Your inner state determines who and what you attract to you. It dictates the very nature of your desires and attachments.

Anxiety, frustration, fear, jealousy, greed, anger, delusion, and conditionality – to be free of these, forever. What's wrong with that!? Nothing.

My Restless Mind

Growing up and well into adulthood my mind was always restless. Having been raised in the Christian religious tradition I did not know the difference between religion and spirituality. Like all of the people whose company I kept, I did not want God or the sublime state of Bliss and *Love without distinctions* that can be experienced beyond the mind and beyond the senses. What I wanted was a notion of God that would conform to my limiting desires and cravings for worldliness – a God that is convenient.

This is a **karmic state of contraction** that I suffered. I fell in and out of intimate relationships with women and was depressed a lot of the time as a result. If it rained, I was depressed. If it got cold, I was depressed. In summer I longed for winter and in winter I longed for summer. I defined myself by how much I was or was not earning at my jobs. I pursued status in order to be praised, and to avoid blame. I drank and smoked, even when I was training in track and field and speed skating and knew it was no good for me (at that time, I wanted to be a great athlete).

I felt government, my parents and my landlord were to blame for the life circumstances that did not meet with the approval of my ego. And when I was unable to fulfill all of my desires and cravings, I blamed God. "What has God done for me lately?" was my thinking. I was full of contradictions. My restless mind was always ruminating over my future and, as a result, I was unable to be fully present in the moment. Even though I chased after pleasure, I wallowed in my pain.

During my career in the Performing Arts, I had spent a good deal of time getting to know the celebrities I performed with. Later, while pursuing business ownership, I was mentored by wealthy business owners who were multi-millionaires. I came to know them personally, and also spent time with their families. At that time, I wanted to have their lifestyles.

What I observed in these people is that, even though they had fulfilled so many of their worldly desires and fantasies, they weren't happy. They did not know peace. When I asked them "What is Love?" they did not have an answer. When I asked, "Are you happy?" they answered "Who is really happy? I'm normal."

Through this experience I decided that the people whose lifestyles I wanted, the people who I had looked up to and wanted to be like for so long, had not attained what I was seeking. So, I decided not to pursue their lifestyles.

It was at this time that I started to ask the questions **Is this all there is? What is fate? What is destiny? Who am I? Why am I here? Why was I born?**

And then I met a very great being, Muktananda Paramahamsa, who became my spiritual leader, my Guru. I took him as my Guru for only one reason: After spending time in his company and observing his speech and behavior, I realized that he lived in a state of complete Joy, Happiness, Fearlessness and Freedom all the time. And this is a state that I wanted. After testing him over a period of time, I determined that he had the ability to lead me in attaining that state.

The Pleasure Garden of This World

I began this introduction by stating that this world is a pleasure garden to roam in with unconditional love, total peace and complete joy. If you don't experience it as such, the reason you don't experience it as a pleasure garden all the time is because you are bound by the pursuit of pleasure in an attempt to avoid pain. This forces you to live in the world of your inner impressions that you have created by way of so many past and present karmas that dictate your mental conditioning.

This is a book about permanent spiritual transformation. Its purpose is to convey why an improved inner state and permanent spiritual transformation are so important for your daily existence – and to give you the methods and necessary steps to permanent spiritual transformation by improving your inner state.

Let's begin.

Chapter 1
What Comprises
Your Inner State?

Your inner state is the sum of all the thoughts that linger in your mind, the impressions left behind on your mind that are then deposited into your memory, along with what you experience if you are able to go beyond your mind and your senses to that Witness to your mind. For example, perceived notions of pleasure and pain, duality and diversity, praise and blame are all part of what I refer to as your inner state. The experience of joy, peace and love without conditions is also part of what I refer to as your inner state.

Here in Nityananda Shaktipat Yoga, we define spirituality as the path to experiencing your God nature and your God power. In this way, spirituality and a spiritual path is the means to go beyond your mind and beyond your senses to experience the indescribable Joy of the inner Self. So, by this definition, any true spiritual path is one in which you understand, through direct experience, that your church is inside you. It is the growing experience that, in my Guru's words, God dwells within you as you.

The most important point regarding true spirituality is that it is a means to decrease the thoughts that linger in your mind, a means to decrease the impressions left behind on your mind while increasing your direct experience of joy, peace and the freedom that comes from knowing and experiencing the elixir of Love – the Love of the true heart. Such a spiritual path is engaged in order to increase, to expand your experience of the indescribable Joy of the Self.

The 4 Pillars of Joy In Daily Living

When I first heard my Guru speak of the possibility of living in a state of Joy, I refused to believe that it was possible. Then, as I applied the daily spiritual practices I was taught by him, I began to experience this Joy more and more. This brought up an obstacle. FOMO. As I began to understand that I was engaged in a direct approach to *permanent* spiritual transformation, a conflict arose in my mind with respect to not compromising my growing experience of the Joy of the true Heart. I began to think that, by engaging in an effective spiritual discipline, I would miss out on something that my friends, relatives, lovers and associates were enjoying in mundane life. This is a *fear* that I have since observed in many of the students who take up the methods and instruction taught in Nityananda Shaktipat Yoga. For this reason, I have framed the spiritual practices I instruct in 4 Pillars of Joy In Daily Living.

These 4 pillars are:

1. The Spiritual Power
2. Improved Mental State
3. Emotional Resilience
4. Vibrant Health

The Spiritual Power is the energy substratum of everything and everyone. We also use the Sanskrit term *Shakti* to refer to it. Here in this Earth plane, everything requires power. We need power to think, to speak and to act. We need power to engage our mundane existence, and power is required to fuel the ideas that then become the building blocks for life in society and the improvements made to mundane living.

The truth is we live on a rock that hangs in a void of space with nothing material with which to hold it there. This rock called "earth" spins back and forth on an axis, in an orbit around a fireball. And no government, no nation, no president or prime minister, no standing army, no sovereign wealth trust, no billionaire, no technology – nothing and no one can change the fact that we live on a rock that hangs in a void of space with nothing material with which to hold it there, spinning back and forth on an axis, in an orbit around a fireball. And this phenomenon has been going on, *in an orderly fashion*, for longer than anyone knows.

This is evidence that there is a sacred law here. And, in the words of Mahatma Gandhi, where there is law, there is a lawgiver. So, there is a sacred law that is evident in the power that gives life to everything and everyone on the planet. That power is a spiritual power that can be harnessed in a way that reveals your God nature and God power – The Spiritual Power. Recognizing and experiencing this power is a necessity for being able to improve your mental state.

The following is taken from a video interview on this pillar.

Pillar 1. The Spiritual Power

Kambra:
Can you talk more about the first pillar in the 4 Pillars of Joy in Daily Living?

Kedarji:
Yes. So here in Nityananda Shaktipat Yoga, we have 4 pillars that frame how instruction is offered, and how people are led in their journey to permanent spiritual transformation, and ultimately, liberation.

The first pillar, we call Chit Shakti, which we refer to as The Spiritual Power. That's the translation. Chit Shakti—The Spiritual Power. And so here in our earthly existence, we need power for everything. We live on a rock that hangs in a void of space, without anything material with which to hold it there, spinning back and forth on an axis in an orbit around a fireball. And this is a phenomenon that has been going on for longer than anyone knows. But it is a fact that we live on a rock that's hanging in a void of space with nothing material with which to hold it there, spinning on an axis back and forth in an orbit around a fireball.

And so, truly speaking, all science has to begin with the observation and the understanding of this phenomenon. Because there's no prime minister, no president, no nation, no drug cartel, no sovereign wealth trust, no standing army— nothing and no one has the ability to manipulate or change this fact: that we live on a rock that hangs in a void of space, spinning on an axis in an orbit around a fireball.

As Mahatma Ghandiji has said, "Wherever there is law, there is a lawgiver." So, we have to, by inference, understand that this Chit Shakti—The Spiritual Power—is indeed the substratum, the energy substratum of everything and everyone.

We need power to think. We need power to speak. We need power to see. We need power to hear. Our bodies rely on power to function. Indeed, this power is the same power, and it's a spiritual power. Even the branch of quantum physics known as quantum mechanics now agrees that an object can be simultaneously something material, while also being an invisible force field wave. This is how it's put.

My Guru said that one day, modern science would catch up and eventually prove what the sages of steady wisdom in our lineage have been saying for millennia. And this has actually happened. So, The Spiritual Power, Chit Shakti, the substratum of everything is, indeed, who we really are. This power embodies our true nature—what we also refer to as our God nature or our God power.

In the first pillar, Chit Shakti, we focus on the methods for people to experience this power as a blessing of indescribable joy. Peace of mind, indescribable joy, the bliss of the Self. We instruct in methods for spiritual practice: First, true meditation. We say true meditation because many people have been led to believe that meditation is reverie on past memories, or visualizing beautiful scenes from memory, or a scene sitting on the beach, or listening to favorite music. I know many, many meditation teachers (so-called) who when the meditation starts, they talk people through the entire meditation. If the meditation is half an hour, the teacher is talking for the entire meditation. That's not meditation.

So, true meditation is that which causes the mind to become quiet and silent, and eventually dissolve. So that's the kind of meditation we teach here: Meditation on the Self. Meditation on that God power. The goal is to experience joy in daily living. Peace of mind is the start. We teach meditation to quiet the restless mind. We teach methods that focus on mantra yoga, japa, mantra repetition, which is an excellent, simple way to begin to quiet the restless mind. We teach chanting, which is a form of japa that combines mantra with the joy of song. We teach selfless service: Learning how to serve others selflessly, without being focused on any reward is an incredibly important part of developing what it is to be human. And then there are the wisdom utterances of the sages of steady wisdom of our lineage, indicated in our sacred texts and scriptures, which we also instruct people to study, and to examine from time to time.

So these are the methods, so that the experience can become, over time, living in an uninterrupted state of Joy. But to do that, you have to understand that the basis for all power that we experience in our mundane existence is this Chit Shakti, The Spiritual Power. So that's the first pillar.

Kambra:
Thank you so much.

Improved Mental State is a state in which you are able to rein in the restless mind in order to experience more and more of the indescribable Joy of your God nature – the Self. The direct experience of Joy enables the recognition that *happiness is a spiritual principle* that *is not* dependent on anything or anyone outside yourself. This recognition goes a long way to understanding the difference between happiness and satisfaction – satisfaction being entirely based on outcomes that you perceive to be pleasing and pleasurable. In this regard, satisfaction is based on the desire to possess people, places and things on some level, to some degree, the outcome of which you find satisfying. This notion breeds attachment and attachment always brings suffering. More about attachment shortly.

The following is taken from a video interview on this pillar.

Pillar 2. Improved Mental State

Kambra: What is the second pillar of this approach?

Kedarji: The second pillar is known as Santosha which means Improved Mental State. And it relies on power. So, there has to be the experience of the first pillar in order to begin to improve the mental state. So, the second pillar is dependent upon the first pillar.

In Santosha, the focus is to, as I said, improve your mental state. We have found through so many case studies that we have done, surveys that we have taken, and also the research that we have done, that most people live with a restless, agitated mind. And this is just a fact. And it's certainly true of everyone who comes to our school.

So, when the mind is restless, when it is agitated, it's impossible to experience peace. It's impossible to experience indescribable joy, the euphoria, the bliss of the Self. For that to happen, the mind has to become quiet. The mind has to become silent. This is not as hard as it may appear. We have methods, and it's very important, to learn how to go beyond your mind and beyond your senses. Beyond the mind, beyond the senses there is the experience of the Indweller, and that's the witness to your mind.

There is a witness to your mind. We ask people, "How do you know you're thinking? How do you know you've slept?"

Often people wake up and they say, "Wow, I had a great sleep." How do you know that, if you were asleep and the mind was mostly inactive, and the brain was inactive? How do you know that you've slept well? So, people often say, "Well, I had a great sleep." How do you know?

And yet you know you're thinking. You know these things because there's an Indweller, a witness to your mind. We frame this in what we call witness consciousness, because there is a spiritual witnessing awareness. And that spiritual witnessing awareness is beyond the mind, and beyond the senses. And the goal is to be able to keep the mind quiet enough to experience that state of witness consciousness. From that state, observations—very important observations—can be made.

First and foremost, it's very important to remember: The mind loves the places it frequents the most. Your mind loves the places it frequents the most. So, this begs the question: Where do you allow your mind to wander? In what nooks and crannies do you allow your mind to go? Because you have the power to direct your mind. Everyone does. Some people don't take responsibility for that fact. Others do. But the truth is, you're responsible for where your mind goes.

And so, if you allow your mind to wander into places that keep the mind restless and agitated, you're never going to experience Chit Shakti— The Spiritual Power. So, part of improving the mental state is learning how to go beyond the mind, beyond the senses first, so that you become aware of where you allow your mind to wander. Because again, the mind loves the places it frequents the most.

My Guru used to say, "If you meditate on lemons, you're not going get mangoes." So that's the first thing. Observing, and having the ability to observe where you allow your mind to go that is no longer useful for your spiritual journey.

Second, you get what you meditate on. This is the second primary focus of improving your mental state and it's really important to understand and embrace this. You get what you meditate on. If you allow your mind to constantly wander restlessly and in an agitated fashion into thoughts, notions, beliefs that are contracting, you're going to remain contracted. Then it becomes almost impossible to experience peace, almost impossible to experience indescribable joy. Because you always get what you meditate on.

So, conversely, if you meditate on the Self, if you meditate on the indescribable joy of your God-nature, now the mind begins to expand.

People make the mistake of thinking that the mind is the brain. These are two separate things. The brain is not the mind. In fact, the mind is the parent of the brain. And the Self, God, is the parent to the mind. This is very important to remember. So, improved mental state means first that you acknowledge that the brain is just a lump of flesh with some nerves sitting in water. The brain is a signaling station for what is sent to it by the mind—the thoughts, the notions, the beliefs that then the brain interprets in ways that signals can be sent to the organs, to the muscles, and to your cells, ultimately. And so, these two are different.

The second point of confusion that's very important to understand if you're going to improve your mental state is that there's a difference between happiness and satisfaction, and this is where people really get stuck. Happiness and satisfaction are not the same. Satisfaction always hinges upon outcomes. Satisfaction hinges upon whether or not you feel you have attained outcomes to a particular level that, quite honestly, satisfies your ego.

Happiness, on the other hand, in order to be happiness, cannot be dependent upon any person, place, thing, or outcome. Cannot. Happiness is a spiritual state. It's an innate state. The reason why people don't understand this is because their minds are too agitated. So as the mind becomes quieter and quieter, and as you develop the ability to turn your mind within, which you have the power to do, and to direct it to the Self, to this state of indescribable joy and peace—because the mind is an energy of consciousness—and so as you do this, the mind begins to expand, and expand, and expand beyond the limitation of restlessness, beyond the limitation of agitation. And with your witnessing awareness, you're really able to begin to see and to experience how important it is to direct the mind to your God-nature. To your God power. Rather than allowing it to wander in useless notions, beliefs, and thoughts.

So that's the second thing: You get what you meditate on. Very important to remember, because if your mind is agitated, you can't complain. It's because you're allowing your mind to meditate on things that keep it contracted.

The third part of improved mental state is to remember always that you become what you obey. You become what you obey. This is absolutely true, and you can observe this for yourself. This is connected, of course, to the fact that the mind loves the places it frequents the most, and you get what you meditate on.

So, if the restless mind is not arrested, if the agitation of the mind is not cured, it's like a self-fulfilling prophecy. So, with an expanded mind, you're actually able to overcome fear, doubt, anxiety, worry, greed—all of these things that keep the mind contracted, that keep the mind agitated, you're able to overcome those.

But if you don't take the steps to improve your mental state, you become trapped in the prison of those things. And this is easy to understand, particularly from the place of spiritual witnessing awareness.

And so, with improved mental state—again—we have methods that are employed that I mentioned previously, and I'll mention again: meditation on the Self, japa, mantra repetition, chanting of mantras, selfless service, and also some degree of study of the wisdom of the Siddhas of our Siddha nation. And in this way, the mind begins to expand. The mind learns how to become quieter and quieter, even during the course of your daily mundane existence.

Now, because you didn't ask me this, but I know you're probably going there: It is often a comment that people who meditate in the way I've described, who use these methods, are simply space cadets—that they just get spaced out, and they're not able to really practically engage in life. And this could not be further from the truth.

A quiet mind is a sharper mind. And this has been proven. There's no doubt about this. And we have case study after case study after case study. A quiet mind is a sharper mind. And as you improve your mental state in this way, something else happens. You have more available mental energy. This is also true. This is Santosha: Improved Mental State.

Kambra: Thank you so much.

The third pillar, *Emotional Resilience*, evolves out of the growing experience of an improved mental state. My Guru used to ask, "Are you enjoying your senses or are your senses enjoying you?" Emotional Resilience is the ability to engage your emotions, to express humanity, without becoming a slave to your emotions. It is entirely possible to express humanity and engage emotions without riding the roller coaster of emotionality.

For example, parents of young children have told me that there have been times when the kids were not listening and following what the parent told them. In that situation, the parents expressed that they had to "up their game." Although they did not want to raise their voices or yell at their children, they realized this was necessary, at times, to get their attention. What has been described to me is that, *while smiling inside*, the parent had a 'ferocious' moment in expressing anger. Indeed, the parent was *playing at being angry* in order to get the child's attention to emphasize what the child was being told. This is an example of emotional resilience that many parents have experienced.

The following is taken from a video interview on this pillar

Pillar 3. Emotional Resilience.

Kambra: What is the third pillar of The Four Pillars of Joy in Daily Living?

Kedarji: The third pillar we call Shakti Bhava—emotional resilience. Shakti Bhava. And of course, this pillar is dependent upon the first two. In order to have emotional resilience, in order to sustain emotional resilience, you have to be able to harness The Spiritual Power and you have to develop an improved mental state.

The emotions are very, very powerful. And so, emotions, if not directed properly, can keep the mind in a prison of agitation. And this, I'm sure you know. Everyone knows this. This is an experience that people have a lot. Because again, what we have found through our case studies, our surveys, and our research is that most people ride the emotional roller coaster. We call this emotional slavery. People are used to riding the emotional roller coaster so much so that there are many people who believe that that's what it takes to be human. They think, "If I'm not riding an emotional roller coaster, I'm not being human."

And this could not be further from the truth. Now it is true, while we are embodied, we are gifted with humanity. And it's very important to express this humanity. This is something that we must do. That expression takes the form of emotions. Now the challenge is to be able to express, to feel the emotions without becoming a slave to them. So, most people exist in a state of emotional slavery, and this is very unfortunate, but it can be quickly cured.

So, the steps that we take in Shakti Bhava to increase emotional resilience—we have a number of methods, but there is a primary method that we utilize that people find very, very helpful. This is called the principle and the practice of the Arc.

The principle is this: The understandings that you reach for and embrace will always dictate how you feel in the moment, and the subsequent emotions that you experience in that moment, from moment to moment. Then feelings, emotions are expressed. They manifest as a result of understandings. So, your understandings dictate how you feel, and the subsequent emotions that are being expressed. And then based on the emotions that are being expressed, that dictates how you're vibrating in the moment—meaning what you're putting out, what you're projecting into Consciousness. And what you're projecting into Consciousness always dictates who and what you attract into your daily mundane existence. Who and what you attract into your life.

Now, every person is responsible for this. And I know so many people who say, "Well, you know, I'm on my third relationship from hell. Why do I have to go through this?" Well, it's because of what you're putting out.

We have a saying here: a yogi's first duty is full responsibility. And with respect to the Arc, it's very important that you take full responsibility for who and what you're attracting into your daily mundane existence. That comes by way of the understanding of this principle of the Arc.

And then there is the practice of the Arc. Extremely important for Shakti Bhava—for increasing emotional resilience. We start with an examination, and that examination is this: most people - and again case studies that we've done, surveys, and our research indicates this - that so many people embrace understandings that they've been given without questioning them. We're raised in this way. And so, the very first step in the practice of the Arc is to sit down and to really bluntly examine: Where have you gotten your understandings from? Parents, teachers, authority figures, friends, associates, lovers, husband, wife, media, popular culture. The list goes on and on.

But the importance of this practice is to really first have a very direct examination, where you determine: What understandings have you accepted blindly without examining, just because they were fed to you? Are those understandings still useful for the direction in which you are headed spiritually, to permanent spiritual transformation—ultimately liberation—are those understandings useful? Because if they're not, you have to discard them.

So, the practice of the Arc is to first examine those understandings. Then to discard understandings that are no longer useful. To be replaced with what? Well, we are very, very fortunate in our Siddha Science that we have sages of steady wisdom who have provided us with wisdom through their utterances. They give us these really great—the highest, purest understandings for our spiritual progress.

And this is where true spiritual leadership comes in. This is a function of two things. First, full Kundalini awakening, which is known as Shaktipat. This is an absolute necessity from the very beginning. And second, to have leadership where you can easily go through this process with respect to the Arc, and begin to discard those understandings that you yourself observe are no longer useful for the direction in which you are headed spiritually.

Some people find this difficult because they think that if they discard useless understandings that they got from their parents, for example, that that's going to put a wedge in their interaction with their parents; or it's going to put a wedge in their interaction with lovers or friends.

You know, I always say this: If the people you're interacting with are truly your friends, they're never going to object to your improving spiritually. That's never going to happen. That only happens when you have surrounded yourself with people who are not true friends. A true friend, even if they don't want to engage in the practices or in the path that you're engaged in, a true friend will always say, "Look, I support you if this is what you want for yourself, and I see you changing. I see you growing. I think this is great."

So, again, with Shakti Bhava, this is the process. You go through it. And you can work the process both ways. You can start with understandings and begin to discard useless understandings, and to embrace more useful understandings, to see how that impacts how you feel, and whether or not you're released from emotional slavery. And then, how that causes you to vibrate. And subsequently, what that does with respect to who or what you attract into your life. And I know from my own experience, this was a complete revelation. Because before meeting my Guru, I was so emotionally enslaved. And I did think that I was this great human being because I could get down in the trenches and be emotionally enslaved, as other people. You know, misery does love company. This is true.

And so, after meeting my Sri Gurudev, I really began this examination in earnest, and I had shocking revelations about how I had reached for and embraced understandings without even examining them. There were understandings that I embraced just because I wanted to be part of a peer group, because I didn't want to suffer peer pressure. There are understandings that I embraced because I wrongly thought that it would bring me closer to a lover or to a friend.

You know there's this old thing that friendship is determined by how many things you like that are similar, right? This is true in love relationships or intimate relationships also. I think, I don't know why, but this is how so many people function. They go down a list; "Do you like this movie? Do you like this music? What did you think of 'Eat, Pray, Love,' because I saw that 250 times. You better not say you don't like it, 'cause then we're gonna have to break up."

But this is the pressure of being emotionally enslaved. So, you can work it this way: From the top, starting with understandings. Or you can start by examining from the other direction— who and what do I continue to attract into my daily existence that is no longer working for the direction in which I want to go? You can start there.

You can say, "Well, this is the tenth relationship from hell. What am I putting out that's causing me to attract these people into my life?" You can start there and work backwards to then examine how you're vibrating that causes you to attract those people, places, and things into your life. And then from there, how you're vibrating, to look at what your emotional state is, and then source out, "Well what are the understandings that have caused me to contract in this way?"

You can work it back and forth both ways. This is the Arc. Shakti Bhava.

I'll end by saying one more thing. If your intention is permanent spiritual transformation, if you want the indescribable Joy of your God-nature, it is imperative that you examine all understandings that you hold. All. This is Shakti Bhava.

Kambra: Thank you so much.

The fourth pillar, *Vibrant Health*, is equally important. The body is the temple in which God resides. For this reason, it is important to keep the body healthy and disease free, and to prepare the body to age gracefully with as few health complications as possible. To this end, in Nityananda Shaktipat Yoga, we have this fourth pillar of Joy.

I hold degrees as a doctor of Eastern and Oriental medicine. I graduated with degrees in both from the Kushi Institute and had a practice in New York City for many years. In addition, I have worked with and studied under many of the world's top doctors, virologists, microbiologists and epidemiologists. Through that extensive period of time I observed that most people have little or no idea of how their bodies function at the cellular level. And most people treat their cars far better than they treat their bodies. The truth is if you don't fix the cell, you will never get well and stay well.

For these reasons, from time-to-time, I have offered a Wholistic Well-Being Challenge that has provided education and support for people to address and heal their illnesses and diseases, while attaining vibrant health through applying a basic knowledge of the ecology of well-being taught in Nityananda Shaktipat Yoga.

The following is taken from a video interview on this pillar.

Pillar 4. Vibrant Health

Kambra: Tell us about the vibrant health pillar.

Kedarji: Jeevant Shareera, which means vibrant health. This is our fourth pillar of the 4 Pillars of Joy in Daily Living. And again, I just want to remind you that this pillar has, as its foundation, the first three pillars. They're all integrated. Jeevant Shareera, vibrant health. Here we understand that the body is the temple in which God resides. Your body is the temple in which you reside. Because you are God, you are the Self, you are That.

I also like to say that the body is like your biological space suit. And I use that analogy for a reason. Astronauts wear space suits. And when an astronaut is getting ready to go into space, they bring out the space suit. Someone has examined the space suit, and then they say, "OK here's your space suit." The astronaut does not just simply put on the space suit. The astronaut examines that space suit down to every small detail. Every astronaut does this. They don't take anybody's word for it. The astronaut knows, "I'm going to put this space suit on. I'm going up into space. If something's wrong with the space suit, I'm responsible, not the person who just told me the space suit is fine, not the person who made this space suit. I'm responsible for catching any problem with this space suit before I put this thing on."

And so that's why I like to use this analogy, your biological space suit, because everyone should be like the astronaut. In our case studies and our research, we find that most people treat their cars and their cell phones better than they do their bodies. It's kind of incredible if you really think about it.

Secondly, most people, the majority of people, have almost no knowledge of how their bodies function. None. What do I mean by that? Well, sure, we're taught some degree of biology in school, but really you have to know how your cells function. If you don't fix the cell, you'll never get well and stay well. This is very, very important to remember. So, our focus in this fourth pillar—and we have a good deal of instruction and leadership that we offer in this regard—the focus is to first help people to understand that, if you're ill, or if you're suffering from a disease, you are responsible for having contracted that illness or disease. Now a lot of people don't like to hear this, and I understand. But again, ultimately, you are responsible for your biological space suit. And if it breaks down, you are responsible for that breakdown.

Now a lot of people say, well you know it's all genetic inheritance. This is not true. This has been debunked. It's absolutely certain now; we know this without a doubt that, as far as illness and disease is concerned, genetic inheritance comprises only 5-8% of all illness and disease. What that means is that 95% of all illness and disease is due to lifestyle. 95% is due to lifestyle. So, in this fourth pillar, Jeevant Shareera, we train people how to make lifestyle changes. Keep in mind, of course this pillar is based on the first three. If you don't have the ability to harness The Spiritual Power, if you don't have an Improved Mental State as a result, if you don't have Emotional Resilience as a result of an improved mental state, you will never stay the course long enough to change your lifestyle.

Lifestyle changes require massive action. Massive action over an extended period of time. I was over 300 pounds at one point. My ideal weight range for my height is 140 to 179. So, I was morbidly obese. Obesity is a gateway disease, by the way. So, as I became morbidly obese, I got sick with other illnesses. I had lung problems, I had problems with my heart, I developed type 2 diabetes which I eventually cured. I had all these other diseases that came on as a result of being morbidly obese. I took my body for granted, and I put things into my body that one should never put into the body. I had a little bit of coffee with my sugar. I had a little bit of fruit juice with my sugar. Things like this. I ate foods that were horrible for my cells and organs, and I did so with great ignorance and with great bliss. I shoved food into my mouth. And the other thing is I was eating constantly.

People eat constantly. The body is not made to be constantly shoving food in the body. Two or three squares a day is enough, and people shouldn't snack in between. It's not good for the blood sugar; it's not good for the cells.

And so, in this fourth pillar, we have instruction and methods that we give to help people change the lifestyle that created the illness. Why do I say this? Because you have to be able to get to the root cause. And most people are just so used to treating the symptoms only. People go through life simply treating symptoms. If you're going to have vibrant health, you have to get to the root cause of what's ailing you. To do that, there's only one direction you need to go, and that's the cell. If you don't fix the cell, you'll never get well and stay well.

So, in this fourth pillar of Vibrant Health, we support people in making the lifestyle changes necessary that are going to support optimal cellular function. Oxphos, it's called. Oxidated phosphorylation. Oxphos. So that the cells are oxygenated and breathing optimally. This requires something called cellular nutrition. Most people simply eat for taste. We've been trained to do that. This is a matter of understanding - go back to the Arc. So, most people are eating in the way that their parents ate, and then that's where we get this wrong understanding about genetic inheritance. People think, "Well you're sick. You got this disease. You inherited it from your parents." That's not what happened. What you inherited is your parents' lifestyle. You were raised on the lifestyle of your parents. That's the issue. That's what has to be changed. And it can be changed effectively.

We look at the cell. So, what's required for optimal cellular function? We know that cells need optimal nutrition. So, what you put into your mouth matters. And it's very important for you to understand how what you eat and drink is going to impact your cellular function. That's the first thing. We have a whole series of instruction about this. To eat for cellular nutrition. And it doesn't mean that you don't eat for taste. You can have taste and cellular nutrition, both. But you've got to eat for cellular nutrition first to optimize the function of your cells.

And then what causes cells to downregulate? What else causes cells to lack function and to eventually go rogue? Well, stress. So now we're back to The Spiritual Power, Improved Mental State, Emotional Resilience. Stress, we know downregulates cells and creates illness. Fear, agitation, worry, doubt, all of those things impact cellular function. Recreational drugs, food, of course, also. I've said that already. All these things impact cellular function. So, I'm saying this again so that you really understand that this is a lifestyle change.

Once the lifestyle changes, it's entirely possible to attain vibrant health. We know through the science of epigenetics. Epigenetics means above genetics. Now epigenetics is a science that is now completely embraced. It's about 25 years old, and epigenetics is based on the fact that if, through lifestyle you change the function of your cells, you can even overcome a great deal, if not most, of any genetically inherited illness or disease.

All of my family on both sides became type 2 diabetic in their late 30s, early 40s. All of them. I lived a lifestyle of my mother, so I developed type 2 diabetes early on in my life. I'm completely cured of it now. Doctors said it would never happen. They said there's no way, because it's a genetic inheritance. It was not a genetic inheritance. It was a lifestyle inheritance—that I was leading the lifestyle, eating the foods I was raised on that my mother ate and enjoyed. That's what I inherited. So, when I learned to change that by way of understanding, and again I'm going to emphasize this for the last time now—is that it's about cellular function.

You've got to understand, every individual has the responsibility of understanding the biological space suit which is optimized by the function of your cells. You have to understand how your cells function. At least a basic understanding of how your cells function, what downregulates cellular function, with respect to your lifestyle. That can be everything from stress to lack of sleep, to the foods you eat, etc. Lack of meditation, lack of japa. So, these things all have an impact.

Once you fix the cell, you can get well and stay well, and even overcome to a certain degree, if not to a great degree, genetically-inherited illnesses. So that is Jeevant Sharira.

Kambra: Thank you, thank you, thank you.

Mastering these 4 Pillars of Joy In Daily Living is essential to improving your inner state.

Superimposition

Superimposition is the presentation to Supreme Consciousness, by the memory, of something previously experienced elsewhere. Memory is a part of the subtle body, also known as the sushumna nadi. Until completely liberated from the bondage of ignorance, until this nadi (spiritual center) is purified, your subtle body is full of impressions that have been left behind on your mind. Over time, these impressions comprise the world of your inner impressions that includes all of the karmic impressions you have collected in past lives and your present life. It is from this world of your inner impressions that you superimpose or project thoughts, notions and ideas in the body of Supreme Consciousness and into your waking and dream states.

Consider and observe this:

1. You have contact with an object that you perceive through your senses. The object is a person, place or thing.

2. The object is actually being reflected in the body of Supreme Consciousness (the Self), even though it appears to be outside of yourself (more about this shortly).

3. When the object is no longer being reflected in the body of Supreme Consciousness, you ruminate over the object and become attached to it or averse to it.

4. This attachment causes desire and craving or disdain and aversion to rise within you in connection with the object.

5. That desire and craving or disdain and aversion creates an impression of the object that is deposited into your memory.

6. Then you superimpose or project that impression from your memory (the world of your inner impressions) back into the body of Supreme Consciousness.

Fear of A Black Hat and Jacket

I'll share a story with you to further elucidate the process I have just shared above. I used to live in an apartment building near Lincoln Center in New York City. I had a friend named Roger who lived across the hall from me with his wife. They loved Opera and had season tickets to all the Opera performances at Lincoln Center. They never missed a performance.

One summer afternoon, as they had entered Lincoln Center Plaza to wait by the fountain until it was time to go to their seats for an Opera performance, they were mugged. The mugger was an African-American male wearing a black leather beret and a black leather jacket. Roger got bruised and the mugger took all their money and all the jewelry they were wearing. Roger was so upset by this incident that he cancelled their subscription to the Opera performances. He told me that Lincoln Center had become a cesspool of crime and he never wanted to go back there again. A week prior to this incident he lauded Lincoln Center as the cultural capital of the world.

Two years passed. I knew how much Roger and his wife loved Opera at Lincoln Center. One day I decided to try something to help them break out of their superimposing. I put on a black leather jacket and a black beret and dark sunglasses. I stepped across the hall and rang their doorbell. Then I started knocking on the door. Roger came to the door and looked through the peephole. Then he started screaming to his wife, "Call the police. The man who mugged us two years ago is standing at our door!" I then put my mouth near the door and said, "Roger, it's me." He opened the door with the door chain on and I removed the sunglasses. He started laughing hysterically and called his wife to the door. When she saw me she started laughing also. Well, they got it. A week later they renewed their season subscription to Opera at Lincoln Center. This incident is an example of superimposition.

The Wooden Bowl

A frail old man went to live with his son, daughter-in-law, and four-year old grandson. The married couple were concerned about taking in an elderly man and, even before giving it a chance, had decided that the frail old man would become a nuisance. *This was their superimposition* from many years of worry about who would have to care for the frail old man.

The old man's hands trembled, his eyesight was blurred, and his step faltered. The family ate together at the same table. But the elderly grandfather's shaky hands and failing sight made eating difficult. Peas rolled off his spoon onto the floor. When he grasped the glass, milk spilled on to the tablecloth. Now, this wasn't as bad as they made it out to be.

His son and daughter-in-law became irritated with the mess. "We must do something about father," said the son. "I've had enough of his spilled milk, noisy eating, and food on the floor." So, the husband and wife set a small table in the corner. There, grandfather ate alone while the rest of the family enjoyed meals together at a separate table. Since grandfather had broken a dish or two, his food was now served in a wooden bowl!

When the family glanced in grandfather's direction, sometimes he had a tear in his eye as he sat alone. Still, the only words the couple had for him were sharp admonitions when he dropped a fork or spilled food. The four-year-old grandson watched it all in silence.

One evening before supper, the father noticed his son playing with wood scraps on the floor. He asked the child sweetly, "What are you making?" Just as sweetly the boy responded, "Oh, I am making a little wooden bowl for you and mama to eat your food in when I grow up and you get old." The four-year-old smiled and went back to work making the wooden bowl.

The words of the boy so struck the parents that they were speechless. Then tears started to stream down their cheeks. Both knew what must be done. That evening the husband took grandfather's hand and gently led him back to the family table. For the remainder of his days, he ate every meal with the family. And neither husband nor wife seemed to care any longer when a fork was dropped, milk spilled, or the

tablecloth soiled. And now grandfather ate out of
the ceramic plates everyone else did.

The habit of superimposing in these ways
is addressed at the root level of thinking. Once
you have adopted an effective, daily spiritual
practice to rein in the restless mind it becomes
easier to observe your mind from that Witness to
your mind. With practice you are able to observe
all the places you allow your mind to wander
that are not useful for the experience of peace
and joy. As you observe your mind in this way, it
will become clear how you superimpose and to
what degree. Then, with the practice of Witness
Consciousness (meditation as the observer) to
increase your spiritual, witnessing awareness,
you will be able to dismantle useless
superimpositions that prevent you from being
fully present in each moment with the outlook of
your Divinity, the Self. This is the first step
toward improving your mental state. More about
Witness Consciousness in the final chapter of
this book.

The Arc

The principle and practice of *The Arc* is a
simple and powerful method taught in
Nityananda Shaktipat Yoga for increasing your
emotional resilience. The principle of The Arc is
this: The understandings you reach for always
dictate how you feel in the moment and the
subsequent emotions that you experience. And
that dictates how you are vibrating in the
moment, what you are projecting into Supreme
Consciousness. And whatever you 'put out there'

in Supreme Consciousness always determines who and what you attract into your life.

The practice of The Arc is to closely examine the understandings that you reach for and embrace, along with where you got those understandings from, so that you can discard the understandings that are no longer useful for your permanent spiritual transformation.

The practice of The Arc begins with a simple examination.

THE ARC LIST EXERCISE

Ask yourself the following: Where have you gotten the majority of your understandings from up until now? Then review the list below and journal the answer, referencing all of the sources on this list that apply to you.

- From parents
- From friends
- From lovers, husband, wife
- From popular culture
- From bosses and work associates
- From other authority figures in your life
- From books, newspapers, magazines
- From movies and TV
- From peer pressure
- From the Internet (including Facebook, Twitter, Instagram and Pinterest)
- From your fears
- From your fantasies
- From outcomes of past situations

Now review your list and ask yourself the following, in each case: Have you accepted understandings connected to the sources on your list without questioning or examining them to determine whether or not they are useful for the greatest experience of your well-being and spiritual progress? If so, why continue to reach for and embrace them?

Once you have your list then begin observing the understandings you reach for in your daily mundane existence so that you can observe how your embracing those understandings impacts your spiritual witnessing awareness and your experience of the Bliss of the Self. Do the understandings you reach for cause you to contract? Or do they support the expansion of your experience of peace and joy in recognition of your God nature? Do the understandings you reach for allow you to express your humanity in the delight of your God nature? Or do they cause you to wallow in fear, anxiety, doubt, worry, anger, greed or illusion?

It's important to observe how the understandings you reach for impact your restless mind. Does your mind become more restless or less restless? You can further examine the impact on your mind caused by the understandings you reach for by closely observing what feelings you are having in the moment and what emotions those feelings are bringing up. Then you can closely observe how that impacts how you are vibrating, what you are projecting into the body of Supreme Consciousness and who/what you are attracting to you as a result. This is the practice of The Arc, working it forward.

You can also work it in the reverse by starting with an examination of who/what you are attracting to you so that you can better understand how you are vibrating, based on the emotions and feelings you cling to that will show you the understandings you are reaching for and embracing.

Embracing the principle and practice of The Arc is essential to your developing emotional resilience. And emotional resilience requires an improved mental state, which requires your increased ability to harness The Spiritual Power. So, you can see how these pillars are indispensably connected.

Vibrant Health

As I stated earlier, the body is the temple in which God resides. For this reason, it is important to keep the body healthy and disease free, and to prepare the body to age gracefully with as few health complications as possible. For this reason, it is important to care for your biological space suit, the body you have travelled here in, so that you can use your physical health to support your permanent spiritual transformation. This requires a basic knowledge of how your cells work because if you don't fix the cell, you'll never get well and stay well. Your cells are the cornerstone of the health of your organs, muscle and tissue.

OBESITY

In this regard, obesity is a gateway disease that forms the foundation for illnesses like diabetes, heart disease, stroke and cancer. Obesity always increases the risk of serious medical conditions. Obesity is commonly defined as having too much body fat. A BMI of 30 or higher is the usual benchmark for obesity in adults. [1]

Another way to measure whether or not you are medically obese is to know the ideal weight range for your height. If you are more than 20 pounds over the top weight of your ideal weight range for your height, you are obese. At 100 pounds or more over that top weight, you are morbidly obese.

For example, I am 5' 10" tall. My ideal weight range for my height is 132 to 173. At one point during my health crisis, I weighed 300 pounds! My weight now hovers at 165-170 pounds.

People living in the United States are the most obese people on the planet. During August 2021–August 2023, the prevalence of obesity in adults was 40.3%, with no significant differences between men and women. Obesity prevalence was higher in adults ages 40–59 than in ages 20–39 and 60 and older. About 74 percent of adults in the U.S. are overweight, according to the CDC. That includes nearly 43 percent who are considered obese. Yet 10 percent of those people don't perceive themselves to be overweight, says an analysis of the data. [2]

We are in the midst of a national obesity crisis, and Americans are getting heavier. This includes 15% of children and adolescents in who are also overweight or obese. And childhood obesity is growing in the U.S. The physiological mechanism causing the increase in obesity is no mystery: Americans eat more calories than they burn, and the excess energy is stored as fat. [3]

As of this writing, according to the CDC, the obesity rate among children and adolescents has grown to 19.7%, which is about 14.7 million young people. [4]

Childhood obesity has become a leading chronic disease for children and has increased considerably in recent years. Roughly one in six youth have obesity, according to the newest available data. The data, from the National Survey of Children's Health, show that in 2022-2023, 17.0% of youth ages 6 to 17 had obesity. [5]

DIABETES

According to the CDC, among the U.S. population overall, crude estimates for 2021 diabetes were:

- 38.4 million people of all ages—or 11.6% of the U.S. population—had diabetes.
- 38.1 million adults aged 18 years or older—or 14.7% of all U.S. adults—had diabetes (Table 1a; Table 1b).
- 8.7 million adults aged 18 years or older who met laboratory criteria for diabetes were not aware of or did not report having diabetes (undiagnosed diabetes, Table 1b). This number represents 3.4% of all U.S. adults (Table 1a) and 22.8% of all U.S. adults with diabetes.
- The percentage of adults with diabetes increased with age, reaching 29.2% among those aged 65 years or older. [6]

HEART DISEASE

The American Heart Association researches heart disease, stroke, and other cardiovascular diseases. AHA presents the following statistics:

• Cardiovascular disease (CVD), listed as the underlying cause of death, accounted for 931,578 deaths in the United States in 2021.
• Heart disease and stroke claimed more lives in 2021 in the United States than all forms

of cancer and chronic lower respiratory disease combined.
• Between 2017 and 2020, 127.9 million US adults (48.6%) had some form of CVD.
Between 2019 and 2020, direct and indirect costs of total CVD were $422.3 billion ($254.3 billion in direct costs and $168.0 billion in lost productivity/mortality).
• In 2017 to 2020 in the United States, 59.0% of non-Hispanic Black females and 58.9% of non-Hispanic Black males had some form of CVD. This race category had the highest prevalence of CVD.
• In 2021 in the United States, coronary heart disease (CHD) was the leading cause of deaths (40.3%) attributable to CVD in the United States, followed by stroke (17.5%), other CVD (17.1%), high blood pressure (13.4%), heart failure (9.1%), diseases of the arteries (2.6%).
• CVD accounted for 12% of total US health expenditures in 2019 to 2020, and CVD accounted for approximately 19.91 million global deaths in 2021. [7]

CANCER

In the United States in 2021, 1,777,566 new cancer cases were reported. In the United States in 2022, 608,366 people died of cancer. 2021 is the latest year for which cancer incidence data are available; 2022 is the latest year for which cancer death data are available. [8] Cancer in the U.S. is increasing every year. [9]
At the very least, for all major diseases, there is an increase in disease among both the youth and adult population. Each and every year more people are getting sicker. And this cannot

simply be attributed to hereditary factors. You cannot have a hereditary epidemic. In fact, only 5% of all disease can be attributed to hereditary factors. The other 95% is due to lifestyle.

Lifestyle Is The Cure

Due to the excellent work of Dr. Bruce Lipton and his medical team, a discovery was made that has changed our knowledge and understanding of what impacts cellular health. The science of this is known as *Epigenetics*, a science that has proved that cells change, grow and mutate based on communication (epigenetic expression) that is taking place both inside the cell membrane and between cells in extra-cellular matrices (in connective tissue and organs). *This epigenetic expression can be altered in many ways, without changing the underlying DNA coding.* **This means that, in fact, disease-causing genes can be switched off and health-promoting genes switched on, regardless of inherited genetic predisposition.**

MEDITATION AND CHANTING

The mind is the child of the inner Self, the brain is the child of the mind, and the body is the child of both. Meditating daily and effectively to quiet the restless mind and the chanting of Chaitanya (live Mantras) for the same reason has a profound and lasting impact on cells of the body, over time. There are so many studies to support this fact, and they can be found through Google. The medical profession refers to this as stress reduction and meditation and chanting are now being recommended for people who are being treated for illness and disease.

In blind surveys and case studies conducted over the last 10 years, our Nityananda Shaktipat Yoga program offering has been proved to deliver results in this manner, beyond the expectations of our students.

For every Nityananda Shaktipat Yoga event, when surveyed at the end of the event, participants are asked, "Do you feel more calm and at peace, with a quieter mind now, as compared to when you first came in the door?" 100% of those surveyed answered YES.

In blind surveys, 2 out of every 3 people report that:

- While being led in our Witness Consciousness Centering methods, they experienced a profound sense of Peace and the 'no mind' state in under 3 minutes.
- Their sense of content and happiness increased in the 90-minutes that they attended a program.
- They experienced a state that they recognized to be beyond the mind, the senses and the emotions.
- As a result of practicing the methods they are taught by Kedarji, they experience that they are more confident that they can access the inner strength necessary to take on life's challenges.
- Keeping the company of Kedarji has opened their hearts and freed them from contracting emotions, restless thoughts and attachments to worldliness.

Shaktipat Blessing Intensives

In exit surveys and post-intensive follow up surveys, 96% of all people who have taken our weekend Shaktipat Meditation retreat report that they have become anchored in a life-changing set of experiences that are the clear proof that they received a profound spiritual blessing of Grace that is undeniable.

Of this group, 90% report that, after a 3-year period, post intensive, they are continuing to apply the principles and practices they learned in these weekend awakening retreats with Kedarji, and are experiencing the following results:

- Increasingly permanent states of peace of mind.
- Increased longing to experience the Bliss of the Inner Self.
- Increasing experiences of Joy and Content as they go about their daily mundane activities.
- Relief from chronic health symptoms.
- An ever-increasing, heightened spiritual awareness that allows them to share Love without conditions, without making distinctions or relishing in the false notion of duality.
- The increased ability to engage their lives without becoming attached or experiencing aversion to people, places and things.
- The steadily increasing ability to take on life's challenges while remaining centered in their experience of inner Peace and Joy.
- A sharper mind and increased inspiration for daily living.

Of this same group, 80% report that, after a 5-year period, post intensive, they are continuing to apply the principles and practices they learned in these weekend awakening retreats with Kedarji to experience the following results, in addition to those stated above:

- The ability to maintain a heightened spiritual awareness, steeped in the experience of inner Peace and Bliss, that is not reduced by worldly distractions or the fluctuation of situations and circumstances.
- A purified heart that is open to giving and receiving without bartering needs for wants.
- A deepening experience of Love without distinctions in all their interactions.
- A quiet mind that dissolves in Bliss and Inner Peace.
- The ability to change their lifestyle to improve their health and well-being.

EAT FOR CELLULAR NUTRITION

The first step in a lifestyle change for vibrant health is to eat for cellular nutrition. You can do so without compromising taste. This does require a basic knowledge of how your cells work, along with foods that downregulate cell function and foods that upregulate cell function. I have created a video-on-demand version of our Wholistic Well-Being Challenge that covers this and more in an online, home study course. You can find information about that here http://bhaktaschool.org/holistic-health-well-being-ohio/.

EAT COMPLEX CARBS

For vibrant health it is essential to understand the difference between simple and complex carbohydrates so that you can stop eating simple carbs and start eating more complex carbs that have a greater nutritional value for your cells. For example, white rice is a simple carb that has had most of its nutrients stripped away because the hull has been removed. This means white rice burns quicker in your body and, as a result, has a higher glycemic load that creates glucose spikes. Whereas whole grain brown rice is a complex carb that retains many more nutrients because the hull is intact. Whole grain brown rice also burns slower and, as a result, has a lower glycemic load (better for your blood glucose levels).

Another example is white, processed sugar. This is a simple carb with almost no nutritive value because white sugar is highly processed. This also means it has a high glycemic load (bad for blood glucose levels). Whole brown sugar or turbinado sugar is better because these are more complex carbs that burn slower with a lower glycemic load. And, where sweeteners are concerned, xylitol, monk fruit and stevia are even better because they are slower burning with a lower glycemic load than other sweeteners, lower than raw brown sugar and honey.

BURN MORE CALORIES THAN YOU EAT

Maintaining your weight with a healthy BMI, remaining in range of the weight range for your height is a matter of burning more calories than you eat. This is accomplished in two, primary ways: Monitor the calorie density of the foods you eat in order to manage the number of calories you take in, and intermittent water fasting. Although exercise is very important for other reasons, exercise *is not* a primary tool for weight loss. Even with an intense workout, you may only burn 1-3 pounds and, depending on your exercise routine, that may not be all fat.

A very good aid in managing the calories you take in is to understand and calculate your basal metabolic rate. This will give you an approximate number for the number of calories you need to eat each day to maintain your current weight and the number of reduced calories you should be eating each day to drop weight and keep it off. You can use an online calculator for this purpose at https://www.active.com/fitness/calculators/bmr. Choose the BMR radio button and complete the required fields to calculate. If you want to know the maximum daily caloric intake to reduce weight, enter a weight in the weight field that is your target weight.

Understanding calorie density also means you need to measure the number of calories of each of the foods you eat, in order to understand your present caloric intake. Once you have a good idea of that number for calories and have adjusted your foods for the caloric intake that is ideal for your health and the weight you want to maintain, you will no longer need to count calories.

You also need to read the labels of the packaged foods you buy to calculate the calorie density of those foods. The means for all this is covered in our online course, the Wholistic Well-Being Challenge. You can find information about that here http://bhaktaschool.org/holistic-health-well-being-ohio/.

GUT HEALTH

A healthy gut microbiome is an important key to securing vibrant health. Your gut is your second brain. It sends signals up the vagus nerve to your brain and the brain sends signals back down the vagus nerve to your gut. Due to the processed foods that so many people eat, along with the GMO foods that so many people eat, many people are suffering from leaky gut. Leaky gut is a condition where the tight junctions in your gut loosen. This is known as dysbiosis. With dysbiosis the gut microbiota is impaired and gram-negative bacteria and other pathogens, including glyphosate, cross the gut-blood barrier and enter the blood stream – rather than being carried out of the body in urine and feces. These same bacteria and pathogens, at times, are sent up the vagus nerve and cross the blood-brain barrier.

Dysbiosis is the root cause of heartburn and most gastrointestinal illnesses. It can also be cured by securing tight junctions in the gut by improving gut health. Maintaining gut health is also very important for securing a strong immune system.

DAILY EXERCISE

Daily exercise is essential for improving your health. Whether you choose to work out in a fitness center or you choose dance classes or brisk walks, the point is to exercise. And it is important to exercise to the intensity that you sweat. When you break a sweat during exercise, you reach the level where your body is generating new stem cells. Stem cells are the mother cells from which all other cells in the body are derived. So, it is important to have and maintain healthy stem cells. Exercise is a good way to accomplish this.

INTERMITTENT WATER FASTING

Intermittent water fasting is an invaluable way to reboot your body at the cellular level. It also causes more healthy stem cells to be created, while ensuring autophagy and apoptosis (the recycling of cell matter and the death of cells that are not functioning properly). Intermittent water fasting also balances blood glucose and assists in healing leaky gut. If done properly, you can put your body into a state of ketosis which is essential for training your body to burn more fat. Ketosis is a metabolic state where your body burns more fat for energy, rather than relying only on glucose from carbohydrates. The benefits of intermittent water fasting are numerous, including the documented healing of some diseases.

If you are new to intermittent water fasting (you eat no food for a period of time and drink only water), you can start by taking all your meals in a 9-hour period and then allowing 15 hours before you take your next meal. This is known as fifteen nines. Once you are able to maintain fifteen nines on a daily basis, then you can consider fasting for longer periods of time, depending on your needs. For most people, it is safe to fast in this way for up to five days at a time. More than that requires being medically monitored.

FORCE YOUR BODY TO BURN MORE FAT

Your cells need glucose (converted sugar) in order to function properly. And your tissues and organs need some degree of fat and protein, but less than most people think. Excess fat is stored in your muscles, arteries and tissue. Forcing your body to burn fat is essential for vibrant health. Intermittent water fasting, monitoring the calorie density of the foods you eat, along with exercise all help to move your body into fat-burning mode. With respect to exercise, weight-lifting helps to quickly convert fat to muscle.

In addition, to get the fat off and keep it off (particularly belly fat which is really bad for your health), it is necessary to force your body into a state of ketosis. There are effective methods for doing this, as well as, measuring ketosis levels. The methods are covered in our online course, the Wholistic Well-Being Challenge. You can find information about that here http://bhaktaschool.org/holistic-health-well-being-ohio/.

PROTEIN

Protein is essential for the proper function of your cells and organs, as well as tissue health. However, with the protein craze fueling the promotion of protein powders, protein bars and protein drinks, people have come to believe that they need far more protein than they actually do. A healthy body derives protein on a daily basis from the autophagy and apoptosis of cells. You get about 25-30 grams of protein a day from these processes. Your body weight in pounds, multiplied by 0.3, minus 25-30 grams will give you the total number of grams of protein your body needs on a daily basis.

Your body is either burning sugar, fat or protein for fuel. Ideally, it's a combination of all three with steps you can take to reduce your reliance on just sugar for fuel. You want to reduce your reliance on sugar for fuel so that you can reduce the excess sugar intake that leads to high blood pressure, high blood sugar and diabetes. It's important to eat for energy and smart blood sugar.

It's also important to understand the difference between dietary protein and the protein that is naturally produced by the body (that 25-30 grams). There are three main groups of proteins used by the body: Effector proteins, receptor proteins and integral membrane proteins. For optimal cellular health, it is useful to have a basic understanding of these three.

CLEAN DRINKING WATER

Clean drinking water is essential to vibrant health. You may have seen the movie *Erin Brockovich*, starring Julia Roberts. It's a movie based on a true story of how an electric company in California poisoned the drinking water of an entire community, causing many people who drank the water from their faucets to develop cancer and other diseases. This movie brought to light a fact that is still prevalent in the United States. There is a clean water crisis in the U.S. Many municipalities do not provide safe drinking water to the tap. To better understand this crisis, you can visit Erin's web site at https://www.brockovich.com/.

It is essential that you take steps to purify your drinking water. You can do so by installing water filtration systems in the plumbing of your home. You can also purchase water filters that attach to the faucets in your home. Most have a lever that adjusts the flow of water so that when you are washing dishes or using tap water to clean counters, etc., you can redirect the running water so that it does not go through the filter. Filters need to be changed when full, but that's a small price to pay for clean water.

Alternatively, you can drink bottled spring water or bottled distilled water. Distilled water is the purest water you can drink. The nutrients removed in the distilling process can be gotten from the foods you eat. Be cautious about the spring water you buy. There have been a number of scandals regarding bottled spring water.

There was the Great Bear spring water scandal where Great Bear advertised that their water came from a running spring in Fulton, New York. Residents of Fulton then reported to the press that the spring had dried up many years ago, and that there was no running spring in Fulton. The scandal bankrupted Great Bear and they sold the rights to use their name and logo to another company. Nestle Corp. eventually purchased and retained the rights to the name.

Then both Nestle and Coca Cola got caught adverting their bottled water as spring water when, in fact, their bottled water was filtered tap water. These companies were forced to change their labeling to reflect this fact. Moral of the story: If you haven't seen the spring with your own eyes, it may not be spring water that you are drinking. And, if you don't trust the company that produces bottled distilled water, you can purchase a distilling machine and make your own distilled water. That is a bit time and labor intensive, but you do have that option.

RESTFUL SLEEP

Restful sleep is uninterrupted sleep. The reason restful sleep is so important is that your body, all the way down to the cellular level is repairing itself while you sleep. Adults need an average of 7-9 hours of restful sleep each night. If you meditate effectively on a daily basis of an hour or more, and you've been doing so for several years, you may find that you need less than 7-9 hours to be fully rested. This is because daily Meditation over an extended period of time also serves to repair the body.

MAINTAIN A HEALTHY IMMUNE SYSTEM

For vibrant health it is essential to acquire and maintain a healthy immune system. The first step in doing so is for you to be educated in all the branches of your immune system and how the immune system works. The immune system can be strengthened by permanent lifestyle changes that include getting off foods that contain glyphosate and other harmful pesticides, reducing or eliminating your intake of packaged food fragments, reducing your exposure to toxins, including EMR, in addition to eating organic/non-GMO foods. There are wholistic supplements you can take that will also boost your immune system.

In a healthy body, the immune system is a very intelligent mechanism that can defeat any virus, harmful bacteria and pathogen, even if the pathogen is a bioweapon. This last point is relevant because, not only is there evidence that

SARS-COV2 was developed as a bioweapon [10, 11] but, in the United States, the current DURC (Dual Use Research of Concern) [12] government policy allows researchers and manufacturers using gain-of-function (GOF) experimentation to develop treatments for pathogens like viruses can also use that experimentation to develop a bioweapon.

This policy has literally turned universities and research organizations engaged in GOF into bioweapons laboratories. Obviously, the DURC needs to be eliminated. And it's all about money. For example, once a natural virus is synthetically altered in a lab, it can be trademarked so that the trademark owner is paid licensing fees and royalties whenever the trademarked pathogen is used in further research and the development of a countermeasure like a vaccine.

BLOOD OXYGEN

Blood oxygen is often overlooked. I'm mentioning this here because I have observed that most people do not know what healthy blood oxygen levels are, nor do they monitor their blood oxygen levels. Oximeters are used to measure blood oxygen levels. It's best not to buy the cheap fingertip meters but, instead to purchase a medical grade meter. I use the HealthTree Handheld Pulse Oximeter, Fingertip Pulse Oximeter. It can be purchased online at https://www.walmart.com/ip/HealthTree-Handheld-Pulse-Oximeter-Fingertip-Pulse-Oximeter-for-Adult-Blood-Oxygen-Saturation-Monitor-with-SpO2-Pulse-Rate/1704266590.

A healthy blood oxygen level is a reading between 97-100%. If you perform an intense workout, the reading may drop to 95%, depending on the intensity of your workout. But it should bounce back up to 97-100% within 1-2 hours after completing your workout. Other than after an intense workout, at no time should your blood oxygen level drop below 95%. Below 95% means you need oxygen. Blood oxygen levels below 90% mean you need to go to the hospital emergency room right away.

In addition to trouble breathing, low oxygen levels are known to cause headaches, chest pain, heart arrythmia, fatigue, dizziness, drowsiness and brain fog, among other symptoms. So, it's important to keep your blood oxygen levels in the healthy range.

Low blood oxygen levels can be caused by a number of factors including smoking, the presence of a virus or other pathogen in your lungs, lung diseases such as COPD and cancer, heart dysfunction and/or disease, extended exposure to toxins, asthma and drug overdoses.

Blood oxygen levels can be increased by breathing fresh air, quitting smoking and performing specific breathing exercises on a regular basis. Once you start to use an oximeter to get an idea of your levels, then you only need to take readings randomly.

ANNUAL PHYSICAL

If your body is healthy and you are under 40 years of age, you can expect changes in your health once you get past 40. So, this is the age where you should start getting annual physicals through your primary care physician. You may have to start sooner than 40 if you have health complications that have developed at a younger age.

Your annual physical should include the Comprehensive Metabolic Panel (CMP), Complete Blood Count (CBC), a Lipid Panel and Hemoglobin A1C (HA1c). In addition, it is useful to get C-Reactive protein tested from time to time so that you have an idea of inflammation levels in your body. A Thyroid panel is also useful if you are having any thyroid related symptoms. It is also important to get tested for Lipoprotein A and Pattern B LDL. This is a test that you only need to have done once in your lifetime. It determines your predisposition to types of cholesterol that make you more prone to heart disease and stroke.

TARGETED TESTING OVER 50

50 years of age is a benchmark for the beginning of deterioration in the cells and organs of the body. This means that at 50 and up, there are additional measures you will need to take to protect your health. At 50 years of age, it is useful to get your essential vitamins and minerals tested. This is in addition to the tests mentioned above for your annual physical.

The other is a prescreening test known as Cologuard that will tell you whether or not it is urgent for you to get a colonoscopy. This is done once each year. Or you can skip the Cologuard test and begin colonoscopies. Provided there is no cancer found, colonoscopies are performed every 5 years to age 60. After that, it's every 10 years, except that over 70, colonoscopies are not recommended because the average lifespan of a human being is 72-77 years of age. So, over 70, if you do have colon cancer, the treatment will likely be worse than the disease, given the quality of life you may have at that age. And that quality of life will likely be impacted by other co-morbidities.

TARGETED TESTING OVER 60

At 60 years of age there are several, common diseases that develop in a majority of the population. The first is Non-Hodgkin's Lymphoma (NHL). The most common NHL that is prevalent among people 60 years of age or older is Chronic Lymphocytic Leukemia (CLL). This is a blood cancer that manifests due to a weakened immune system that causes the bone marrow to churn out excess white blood cells prematurely. Another common lymphoma in this age group is Myeloma lymphoma. Myeloma lymphoma is a type of blood cancer that develops from plasma cells in the bone marrow. Myeloma lymphoma is often called multiple myeloma because most people (90%) have multiple bone lesions at the time it is diagnosed.

These diseases are diagnosed by a Hematologist who is also an Oncologist. The diagnosis is determined by specific blood tests, the main one being the CBC with differential. If diagnosed with any of these, there are both wholistic alternatives and standard approaches to treatment that extend life and, in some cases, cure the disease.

Osteoporosis is another common medical condition in the over 60 group. Bones become brittle and porous. This means people with osteoporosis are more prone to fractures and bone breaks, requiring caution in moving around and exercising in a way that puts undue pressure on bones and joint. Osteoporosis is diagnosed with a bone density test which is a type of Xray.

The other common medical condition in this age group is Osteoarthritis which occurs when the cartilage in joints like the shoulders, knees and hips deteriorates and disappears, causing a condition known as bone on bone. Often, this is due to injury, but it can also occur, in part, due to the presence of other conditions that impact cartilage and blood flow to the joints in some way.

This condition is diagnosed through Xray. People with Osteoarthritis can live with the condition and get regular physical therapy that is designed to strengthen the muscle, ligaments and tissue around the joints to take direct pressure off of the joints, while increasing flexibility. The only other alternative to addressing this condition is to have joint replacement surgery.

Chapter 2
What Is Permanent Spiritual Transformation and Why Is It So Important for Your Daily Existence?

Permanent spiritual transformation is a growing state of peace, stillness and ever-increasing Joy. It is an inner state in which you are able to experience and express the fullness of humanity in an increasing state of delight in the inner Self. With permanent spiritual transformation, your mind becomes quiet and sharper, with greater mental clarity. And you begin to experience the expansion of the 4 Pillars of Joy In Daily Living, on a daily basis. From this state, Liberation is entirely possible.

In our modern-day world there are so many distractions and so much noise. Indeed, in the present age, there are two ways to live. One is in a state driven by the restless mind and colored with conflict brought about by attachment and aversion to people, places and things. The other is a state of peace and content, the foundation for which is a quiet mind and the ability to Love unconditionally, while basking in Joy.

The Restless Mind

The mind loves the places it frequents the

most, you get what you meditate on, and you become what you obey. In order to calm the restless mind, it is also important to understand the difference between happiness and satisfaction. Satisfaction is what you experience when your expectations are met or exceeded. In this way, satisfaction is an impermanent state that is entirely dependent on outcomes and your perceived ability to manipulate and control outcomes. Happiness is a spiritual principle and experience. For happiness to be happiness it cannot be dependent on anything or anyone outside yourself. It is an inner experience that has Joy as its foundation.

"The mind is the body of the Self"
~ Muktananda Paramahamsa

It is important to understand that the mind is not the brain. For example, you know this because, even while sleeping, when your brain is inactive, your mind is active in reviewing impressions left behind on it. This is the state of dreaming. The brain is a piece of flesh with nerves in it. And when the water your brain floats in interacts chemically with those nerves, it becomes a switching point that translates information sent to it by the mind into signaling that is then sent to your nervous system, cells, organs and tissues so that your body can function properly.

"Try to understand the mind. The mind is not something you can grab in your fist like a hunk of hair. The mind is nothing but a throb of consciousness." ~ Muktananda Paramahamsa

The mind is an energy of Supreme Consciousness, an expression of the Shakti power that manifests, sustains and withdraws the universe of all the worlds. Your mind is the internal screen on which the manifestation of people, places and things occurs, is then sustained and then withdrawn back into that pure Consciousness, the Self.

"Are you aware of the minds enormous power? From morning until night, it keeps breeding thoughts and images. It never stops thinking new worlds into being." ~ Muktananda Paramahamsa

The world that we experience in our daily mundane existence is a product of thought. It is the creation of the mind. We create our own world by our own thoughts. And thus, we make our own heaven and our own hell. What we experience in the mind is brought about by the conjoining of letters and syllables into the mantras (words) that form sentences that are the foundation for our language.

This conjoining of letters and syllables into mantras is known in Shaivism as *Matrika* [1] or *Matrika Shakti*. It is also called *Matruka*, meaning the un-understood mother of the universe. The mind manifests by way of the Matrika, the conjoining of letters and syllables into words and sentences. In a restless mind, thinking goes on all the time, often completely uncontrollable. For this reason, the mind must be directed inside to the inner Self in order to become calm, quiet and silent.

WITNESS CONSCIOUSNESS

How do you know that you are thinking? When you wake up in the morning and think, "I had a great sleep," who or what is it that observed you sleeping? How do you know you have slept? There is a witness to your mind that exists beyond the mind and beyond the senses. In Nityananda Shaktipat Yoga we refer to this witness as the *indweller*, the *Supreme I-Consciousness* [2]– also known as the *Supreme I-principle* that vibrates as Supreme Consciousness.

You can only really know the mind by observing it from that place of the witness, that place where the mind is observed as it manifests, is sustained and then withdrawn back into the Supreme I. That "I" is always present in our thinking. We say, "I knew," "I ate," "I want to rest," "I see," etc. The Supreme I vibrates as the mind and is the power behind the mind. It is itself an expression of the formless Absolute, the inner Self.

THE MIND LOVES THE PLACES IT FREQUENTS THE MOST

You are responsible for where your mind wanders. In order to rein in the restless mind, it is important to remember that the mind loves the places it frequents the most. The mind that frequents anger begins to love being angry. The mind that frequents fear and cynicism comes to love these. And the mind that frequents the indescribable Joy of the Self comes to love going to That.

Using the heightened witnessing awareness of Witness Consciousness, you are able to observe all the places that you allow your mind to wander into. This is the first step to quieting the restless mind. As you observe where your mind goes, you can begin to redirect your mind inside to the Self. There are simple but powerful methods for doing so that are offered in Nityananda Shaktipat Yoga. As you practice these methods, your spiritual witnessing awareness expands and expands.

It is also essential to understand where everything that you experience takes place. The majority of people assume that there is an outer world in which they experience people, places and things as separate and set apart from themselves. So, here is a question that I put to you as a hypothesis. In science, a hypothesis is a statement/theory that one attempts to disprove first. Because if the theory cannot be disproved then it is embraced as likely being true or absolutely true.

Here is the statement: **There is no outer world. Everything that you experience you experience inside yourself, within the body of Supreme Consciousness.** Here is the question: **Can you disprove this statement? Put another way, can you prove that when you experience a person, place or thing you are having that experience outside yourself in an 'outer world'?**

If you can disprove the statement, please contact me. Because in all my years and that of my Guru, no one has been able to disprove the fact that there is no outer world. Everything that we experience we experience inside ourselves, within that Supreme Consciousness. *And once you accept this to be true, you have to also accept that you are fully responsible for everything that you experience in your interactions with people, places and things.*

We have a saying here that a yogi's first responsibility is full responsibility. You carry around a pot of karmas that you have created in so many past lives and your present life. This pot of karmas dictates your mental conditioning that is the source of all your thinking. The purpose of any true spiritual practice is to 'uncondition' yourself so that you can be freed of your past and present karmas, and so that you stop creating more karmas for yourself that have to be suffered. For that to happen, it is necessary for you to recognize and understand where everything takes place. Because the mind loves the places it frequents the most.

YOU GET WHAT YOU MEDITATE ON

There was a man who was very depressed. He felt that he could do nothing right and that everything in his life was going wrong. He was unhappy all the time. One day he decided that he would leave his house and walk and walk until he finally dropped dead.

So, he marched out his front door and began walking very fast. He continued walking for miles and miles, without stopping, even though he had tired. Suddenly, he heard footsteps behind him. So, he began walking faster. When he sped up, the footsteps he heard speed up. Then he decided to slow down. When he did so, the footsteps behind him slowed down. Finally, he turned to see who was following him.

The man following him said, "I know your predicament and all that you have been going through. If you follow me, I will take you to a place where you can change everything to get whatever you want. The stranger took the lead and the man followed. After a while, they arrived at a big, tall tree in a vast field. The stranger told him to sit under that tree, that it was a wish-fulfilling tree. Whatever he wished for while sitting under that tree, he would get.

The man was excited. He sat under the tree, closed his eyes and began to meditate. He began to feel a tingling moving up his spine. He felt very good – better than he had at any point in his life. Then he began to meditate on all that he wanted. He thought, "I want a huge mansion with many rooms and flower gardens and tree groves." The minute he had the thought a thirty-room mansion appeared. And there were many, beautiful flower gardens and tree groves.

The man was amazed. He began walking around inside the mansion. There was so much space. Then he thought, "Who is going to maintain this place and clean and care for everything? I need a staff of attendants, gardeners and chefs." The moment he had this thought a full staff of attendants, gardeners and chefs appeared. The man was overjoyed.

Then he thought, "Am I really going to live in this huge mansion by myself!? No. I want a gorgeous, sexy young woman to share this place with." The moment he had that thought a young, gorgeous, sexy woman appeared before him. There they sat under that tree together. The man ordered the chefs to prepare and serve them a five-course meal. As the chefs brought the food out, the couple started feeding the food to each other. "How romantic," he thought. "This is everything I have ever dreamed of."

Then the man had another thought. "How is all this possible? How can all this be happening to me? Something is not right." After looking around at all that had manifested, the man thought "No, no, no. This can't be right. Someone is trying to trick me! This must be the work of a demon!" At that very moment a huge demon with big teeth and fangs appeared. The demon devoured the man and spit out his bones. *You get what you meditate on.*

Your past and present karmas are the foundation for your mental conditioning. That conditioning causes habits to form, some of which are not useful for attaining permanent spiritual transformation. Your mental conditioning is also the source of your restless mind and your lack of awareness of the Self and the Shakti of the Supreme.

That Shakti is the energy substratum of everything and everyone. But if you are not aware of this, you are unable to direct your restless mind back to that power source, the purpose of which is to utilize that Shakti to elevate your awareness and experience of eternal joy and freedom. The restlessness of your mind is directly connected to your habit of superimposing that I addressed in Chapter 1, along with lack of emotional resilience that was addressed in the same chapter.

PURIFICATION OF THE MIND

The first step in freeing you from the prison of the restless mind and lack of awareness of your God nature, the Self, is to purify the mind by making the mind quiet. This begins with strengthening your spiritual witnessing awareness as part of Witness Consciousness. This requires a strong and effective daily meditation practice, along with the ability to properly perform contemplation. Here in Nityananda Shaktipat Yoga, we begin with the practice of Witness Consciousness Centering which is a powerful method for stilling the mind in under 3 minutes. This method is discussed further in the final chapter of this book.

Once the restless mind is purified of its restlessness, you will be able to strengthen your practice of The Arc (see Chapter 1) in order to increase your emotional resilience. This is essential to supporting the purification of the mind so that you are able to think of only the highest, by remembering your God nature and experiencing your God power, the Shakti of the Supreme, on a regular and then constant basis.

YOU BECOME WHAT YOU OBEY

Observing all the places that you allow your mind to wander is essential to reining in the restless mind. One of the things that you will observe is that the mind, as an energy of Consciousness, has the power to merge with the objects (people, places and things) that it focuses on. The energy of the mind is a reflective power, reflecting the power of the Absolute. When focused on objects of sense by way of consistently calling the object into your conscious awareness by its name, this reflective power causes the mind to merge with the object of your desire, becoming that person, place or thing.

Due to consistent rumination, impressions are left behind on your mind connected to the object (a person, place or thing) that you then superimpose back into the body of Supreme Consciousness. This superimposing fuels more limiting desire and craving for the object, thereby creating more attachment and attraction to it. Once attached in this way, the ego compels you to obey your desire and craving for the object. This compulsion is very subtle, often operating just beneath the level of your conscious awareness. *In this way, you become what you obey.*

A CONTEMPLATION

To contemplate means to steadily regard with your heart, without prejudging or forming premature notions about that which you are contemplating. Contemplation is the act of using the form to experience the formless. It is the process of perceiving God through the pure perceiving awareness of the Self, contained inside you.

Here is a contemplation that you can perform.

Recall an ongoing attachment to a person, place or thing into your mind now. This person, place or thing should be connected to a desire or craving that you have.

See what you are contemplating on your internal screen. Just hold it there in your awareness, passively, without any reaction or response whatsoever.

To the degree that you are aware, list the driving desires and cravings behind your attachment. Highlight those on your list that are the strongest, meaning the most repetitive.

Now, repeat the Mantra *Om Namah Shivaya* three times and the journal whatever you observed and experienced performing this contemplation.

The Story of
King Khottha

This story is taken from the great sacred text, the *Yoga Vashishtha*. It is from the dialogue between the Sadguru Vashishtha, and his disciple, Rama. Vashishtha once shared the following with Lord Rama:

"There lives a mighty King called King Khottha who is capable of conquering the three worlds. The deities presiding over the worlds faithfully honor his commands. No one can even catalogue his innumerable deeds, which were productive of both happiness and unhappiness. His valor could not be challenged by anyone using any weapon whatsoever, or even by fire, any more than one can hit space with a fist. Even Indra, Vishnu and Rudra could not equal him in his enterprises.

This king had three bodies which had completely engulfed the worlds: and they were respectively the best, the middling and the least. This king arose in space and got established in space. There the king built a city with fourteen roads and three sectors. In it were pleasure gardens, beautiful mountain peaks for sports and seven lakes with pearls and creepers in them. In it there were two lights which were hot and cold and whose light never diminished.

In that city the king created several types of beings. Some were placed above, others in the middle and yet others below. Of them some were long-lived and others short-lived. All this was created by the Maya or illusory power of the king. Here, the king besports himself, with all the ghosts and goblins (who are afraid of self-inquiry or investigation) that had been created to protect the mansions (the different bodies).

When he thinks of moving, he thinks of a future city and contemplates migrating to it. Surrounded by the ghosts he runs fast to the new abode after leaving the previous one, and occupies the new city built in the fashion of a magic creation. In that again, when he contemplates destruction, he destroys himself. Sometimes he wails, "What shall I do? I am ignorant, I am miserable." Sometimes he is happy, at others pitiable.

Thus, he lives and conquers, goes, talks, flourishes, shines and does not shine. Thus, this king is tossed in this ocean of world-appearance.

Thus, has been illustrated the creation of the universe and that of man. Khottha, who arose in the great void, is none but a notion or an intention. This notion arises in the great void of its own accord and dissolves in the great void of its own accord, too. The entire universe and whatever there is in it is the creation of this notion, or intention, and nothing else.

In fact, even the trinity (Brahma, Vishnu and Rudra) are the limbs of that notion. That intention alone is responsible for the creation of the three worlds, the fourteen regions and the seven oceans. The city built by the king is nothing but the living entity, with his different organs and their characteristics. Of the different kinds of beings thus created, some are in a higher region and the others are in lower realms.

Having built this imaginary city, the king placed it under the protective care of ghosts: these ghosts are the ahamkara (ego sense). The king thence-forth sports in this world, in this body. In a moment he sees the world in the waking state, and after some time he abruptly shifts his attention to the world within, which he enjoys in his dreams. He moves from one city to another, from one body to another, from one realm to another.

After many such peregrinations he develops wisdom, getting disillusioned with these worlds and their pleasures and reaches the end of his wandering by the cessation of all notions. In one moment, he seems to enjoy wisdom, while the very next moment he is caught up in pleasure-seeking, and in an instant his understanding gets perverted, just as in the case of a little child.

These notions are either like dense darkness (and give rise to ignorance and births in the lower orders of creation) or pure and transparent (and give rise to wisdom, drawing one close to the truth) or impure (and give rise to worldliness). When all such notions cease, then there is liberation.

Even if one engages oneself in every other sort of spiritual endeavor, even if one has the gods themselves as one's teachers, and even if one were in heaven or any other region, liberation is not had except through the cessation of all notions. The real, the unreal and the admixture of these two are all but notions and naught else; and notions themselves are neither real nor unreal. What then shall we call real in this Universe?

Hence, give up these notions, thoughts and intentions. When they cease, the mind naturally turns to what is truly beyond the mind - Infinite Consciousness. When, in the Infinite Consciousness, Consciousness becomes aware of itself as its own object, there is the seed of ideation. This is very subtle. But soon it becomes gross and fills the whole space, as it were.

When Consciousness is engrossed in this ideation, it thinks the object is distinct from the subject. Then the ideation begins to germinate and to grow. Ideation multiplies naturally by itself. This leads to sorrow, not to happiness. There is no cause for sorrow in this world, other than this ideation" [3].

This story is a perfect example of the fact that you are responsible for your inner state, you and no one else.

The Difference Between Happiness and Satisfaction

In order to set a strong foundation for permanent spiritual transformation, it is necessary to understand the difference between happiness and satisfaction. In fact, so many people confuse satisfaction for happiness, and this keeps them contracted in a state of fear and restlessness.

Satisfaction is what you experience when an outcome that you hope to possess meets or exceeds your expectations. If the outcome meets or exceeds your expectations, you are satisfied and you call that happiness. If the outcome does not meet your expectations, you are 'unhappy' about that.

Happiness, on the other hand, is a spiritual principle. In order for happiness to be happiness it cannot be dependent on anything or anyone outside yourself. This means that you are happy despite expectations of outcomes and regardless of situations and circumstances that come and go in your existence here. *Only this is happiness*, and happiness is the direct experience of the eternal, indescribable Joy of the Self, your God nature, that is evident at all times when you direct your mind to the Self.

This is that state to be had. It is a state of total freedom that makes your spiritual transformation permanent.

Chapter 3
There Is No Outer World

When you experience a person, place or thing, where does that experience take place? Isn't it true that you have that experience inside your own being, within Consciousness?

Nityananda Shaktipat Yoga is a science. We refer to it as Siddha Science, the science studied and perfected by the Siddhas, the God-realized beings of our lineage. Our Siddha Science encourages critical thinking in order to test the wisdom utterances of the Siddhas in the laboratory of our own existence. This means that the understandings imparted to us by these great beings are tested, just as a scientist tests a hypothesis in the laboratory, while recording the outcome of the test.

As stated in Chapter 2, in science, a hypothesis is a statement/theory that one attempts to disprove first. Because if the theory cannot be disproved then it is embraced as likely being true or absolutely true.

Here is the statement: There is no outer world. Everything that you experience you experience inside yourself, in the body of Supreme Consciousness. Here is the question: Can you disprove this statement? Put another way, can you prove that when you experience a person, place or thing you are having that experience outside yourself in an 'outer world'? In all my years and that of my Guru, *no one has been able to disprove the fact that there is no outer world.* Everything that we experience we experience inside ourselves, in the body of

Supreme Consciousness, reflected on the internal screen of the mind.

Until you understand this from your own direct experience, you cannot attain permanent spiritual transformation and your experience of the Self and the eternal Joy and Peace of that experience will be fleeting at best.

The World of Your Inner Impressions

I suggest you take a few minutes to review the section on superimposition from Chapter 1, before you continue here.

Until you are freed from the play of the Gunas and the Malas, you will always have a world of inner impressions that have been left behind on your mind and deposited into your memory. This world of inner impressions is created by way of what Shaivism refers to as the Matrika Shakti, also known as Matruka – the un-understood mother of the Universe.

MATRIKA SHAKTI

Matrika Shakti is responsible for the conjoining of letters and syllables into the mantras (words) that form the sentences of our language. You are able to perceive objects in Consciousness only by calling their name. Calling their name, using their label, occurs when you allow letters and syllables to conjoin into the label, the name for the object (a person, place or thing). It is the mantra for the object that causes that object to manifest in that body of Supreme Consciousness, reflected on the internal screen of your mind. Furthermore, the labels for these objects have a host of understandings connected to them that cause them to appear separate from each other, although they are one and the same in God.

For example, banana is a name for a particular fruit. There are understandings about this fruit that are connected to its label, banana. Understandings like it has a sweet, distinctive taste and is fibrous. It has seeds in the center and has a yellow covering that has to be peeled away before eating the fruit. Hence another label, banana peel. Jalapeño pepper is also a fruit. (Any food that has seeds in it is a fruit.) Understandings connected to this fruit are its green color, hot and tangy taste, hot tasting seeds and the fact that it does not have to be peeled to be eaten or cooked with. This fruit is less dense than a banana.

You call banana and jalapeño pepper into your mind by their names. And it is the understandings connected to banana and jalapeño pepper that cause them to appear separate and different in Supreme Consciousness (the Self), even though they are one in the same in the Self. This is so before you have ever tasted either and more so after you have done so.

To understand the power of the Matrika Shakti used in this example, you can perform the following Dharana (contemplation).

Sit quietly and draw your breath, inhaling slowly and steadily and then exhaling slowly and steadily. Do this three times and then breathe normally as you maintain the awareness of your breath.

Now, call banana into your mind by its name. If it helps, you can also recall the form (image) of a banana into your mind. As the banana forms in your mind, remove the image of the banana from your mind and remove the letters b-a-n-a-n-a from your mind, either all at once or one at a time. Observe what happens next as you follow any sensation you experience back inside. Record what you experience and observe in your journal. This is your scientific record.

Another contemplation: Begin to call a jalapeño pepper into your mind now, by its label. This time, as you do so, and before any image can form, dismantle the mantra j-a-l-a-p-e-ñ-o p-e-p-p-e-r, by either removing the mantra from your mind all at once or letter by letter. Observe what happens next as you follow any sensation you experience back inside. Record what you experience and observe in your journal. This is your scientific record.

Were you able to remove the mantras banana and jalapeño pepper from your mind, along with any corresponding images?

If so, did you experience your mind becoming quiet and then dissolving? Did you experience the banana and jalapeño pepper disappearing from your mind when their names were no longer present in your mind?

Performing Dharanas takes some practice. It is a worthwhile practice for making essential observations about the world of your inner impressions.

THE PLAY OF THE
GUNAS AND THE MALAS

There are impurities planted in your Consciousness. The purpose of them being planted there is to drive you back to oneness with God. This is similar to lifting weights, using the weights as an obstacle to tear-down your muscles so that they heal in a way that they become stronger. The weights, in this example, are the necessary obstacle.

There are three Gunas and three Malas. The Gunas are constitutive properties of nature that form the foundation for all the forms in this universe. They cannot be destroyed while you are in the body, but you can rise completely above their influence. These Gunas are Tama Guna, Raja Guna and Sattva Guna.

The main qualities of Tama Guna are dullness, procrastination and a tendency toward dark and evil thinking. The main qualities of Raja Guna are the compulsion to achieve worldly goals, the tendency to identify those achievements with who you are in order to be recognized for them, and the desire to manipulate and control outcomes and people, places and things on some level, to some degree. The main qualities of Sattva Guna are the desire for a personal relationship with God and the desire to protect/uphold Dharma (righteousness), ethics and morality. Until Liberated, at any given time usually two of these three are at play in your Consciousness, with one being more predominant than the other.

The presence of the three Gunas gives rise to the three Malas. Overtime, these Malas can be destroyed. They are Anava Mala, Mayiya Mala and Karma Mala. Anava Mala is that impurity that causes you to believe that you are just a person, just the mind, the body and the senses with a given name. Anava Mala gives rise to Mayiya Mala. Mayiya Mala causes you to believe that you are unique and set apart from all other people, places and things on the planet. It also causes you to believe that duality and diversity actually are real. Mayiya Mala gives rise to Karma Mala. Karma Mala is that impurity that causes you to believe that, as a person in a body you are the doer of things and that you have the right to possess outcomes and people, places and things that you attribute to your doership.

Here we define doership as the notion that you, as the body, mind and the senses, with a given name are the one doing, in the hope of possessing outcomes. This notion gives rise to egoism.

In order to attain permanent spiritual transformation, the three Malas have to be destroyed, and you have to rise above the influence of the three Gunas. This happens by way of the performance of Sadhana (daily spiritual practice) that is instructed by a living Siddha Guru. The receipt of Shaktipat is also a necessity.

The reason it is so important to understand the Gunas and the Malas and how they play in your Consciousness is that the Gunas and the Malas form the foundation for the world of your inner impressions. Their play results in the karmas that dictate your mental conditioning over a period of many lifetimes. Those karmas are the basis for the world of your inner impressions.

Because this is so, it is essential that you stop running the maze. You have been a maze runner for so many lifetimes. Even if you get the cheese, you're still stuck in the maze. The mouse is ushered into the maze and desperately hunts for the cheese, running the maze back and forth in search of the cheese. It never thinks to stop chasing the cheese and, instead, to find its way out of the maze. Worldliness is like this. This is why the Siddhas of our lineage refer to the play of the Gunas and the Malas as *the prison of the Gunas and the Malas.*

The Mind and The Brain

As I stated in Chapter 1, the mind is the child of the inner Self, the brain is the child of the mind, and the body is the child of both. *Here it is important to understand that your mind is not your brain.* The mind is actually an energy of the Self, God. Your mind comes into being at the moment you allow letter and syllables to conjoin into the words and sentences that form your thoughts. When you have no thoughts in your mind, the mind dissolves. As you are able to increase your witnessing spiritual awareness, you will observe this for yourself.

All notions, all ideas and all obstacles to your permanent spiritual transformation are of the mind and the mind only. Therefore, the restless, wandering mind must be addressed and made to become quiet. This is the only way to begin addressing the world of your inner impressions, by way of purifying the subtle body of those impressions. This requires daily spiritual practice under the leadership and instruction of a living Siddha Guru who has removed these obstacles within his/herself. I discuss this further in later chapters in this book.

Chapter 4
What Is Karma and
How Are Karmas Created?

      The mantra "karma" means action or activity. There is the activity that takes place by God's will. That activity is evident in nature, as well as the fact there is a sacred law here that produces the phenomenon whereby we live on a rock that hangs in a void of space with nothing material with which to hold it there. This rock called "earth" spins back and forth on an axis, in an orbit around a fireball. And no government, no nation, no president or prime minister, no standing army, no sovereign wealth trust, no billionaire, no technology – nothing and no one can change the fact that we live on a rock that hangs in a void of space with nothing material with which to hold it there, spinning back and forth on an axis, in an orbit around a fireball.

      Then there is the activity produced by the thinking of each individual and the collective thinking of a group, society or nation. This type of activity manifests by the will of these embodied beings and, until addressed, is governed by the play of the Gunas and the Malas. The foundation for that play is the false notion of individuality in which you, as an embodied being, come to believe that you are just a person, just the mind, body and senses. This notion, coupled with your belief that you have to become somebody in the eyes of others, and that your identity is caught up in how well you can manipulate and possess outcomes – this gives rise to egoism.

It is the presence of egoism in your thinking and activities that causes you to believe that you, as the body, mind and the senses have the right to possess outcomes on some level, to some degree. It is this notion, based on your individual will, that is the mechanism for the activity you engage that creates your karmas.

In this regard, *it is essential to understand that thought is action.* The body has no agency. It functions by way of how the mind directs it. So, it is at the level of thinking that you create karmas for yourself.

Your Act of Concealment

When you don't have the direct experience that you are God, when you don't know that you are the Self, you are engaged in concealing your true nature from yourself. This act of concealment fuels the ego idea, and you come to believe that you are just a person, just ordinary or delightfully weird. Again, it is in this way that your karmas are created.

THREE TYPES OF KARMAS

There are three types of karmas [1]:

Prarabdha – these are the karmas from previous lives that become the birth reason for your present life. Prarabdha karmas cannot be destroyed. They must be suffered.

Aprarabdha – these are the karmas that are stored in your subtle body that have not yet begun to bear fruit. They will manifest later in your present lifetime or in a future lifetime. These karmas can be destroyed before they manifest. Later in this book you will be taught the basics of how that happens.

Together, the prarabdha and aprarabdha karmas are your karmashaya, your pot of karmas that you carry around with you from birth to death, over and over again. The karmashaya is the foundation for your mental conditioning.

Collective Aprarabdha – these are the collective karmas that form when a group, society or nation thinks in the very same way, thereby manifesting activity that is then suffered by that group, society or nation. An example of this is the Nazism perpetrated by the Nazi party that led Germany and its people to allow mass extermination of Jewish people. Another example is the collective thinking that led to the establishment of Liberty under a Constitution that has protected the God-given rights and civil rights of people living in the United States.

There are no good or bad karmas. There is just karma that then must be suffered until the mind is purified in such a way that thinking is transformed into recognition of God in everything and everyone, everywhere. This brings the understanding and direct experience of the Play of the Shakti as this world. More about this in later chapters.

THE ROOT CAUSE OF KARMAS

Maya means illusion. In Shaivism, we refer to this as Shiva's Maya, due to the understanding that the illusion of a world is created by God. At the foundation of Maya is your free will. Your free will is limited to two choices. You can either follow God's Will for your existence here, or you can neglect to learn of God's Will for your life or ignore that will and, instead follow your will which is based on the false notion of individuality.

In Shiva's Maya, the free will of the individual further serves to conceal God's true nature through the creation of *Karma*. Remember that karma is limiting desire and craving, borne of thought. And karmic law requires that every human wish held firmly in the mind and mixed with devotion must find ultimate fulfillment. This act of concealment unfolds in the following way:

1. Your thinking is caught up in notions and limiting desires and cravings for this and that.

2. This type of thinking traps you in the realm of cause and effect.

3. Your free will, being directed to your false notion that you are just a person or individual, and mixes with the limitation of your ego.

4. This combination causes you to conceal your true nature from yourself.

God will fulfill every desire you have and continue to entertain. If you have the skill to manifest all your desires quickly, you may be able to experience their fulfillment in this lifetime, depending on how many there are. For those who have a lot of limited desires (karma) and little or no skill, they will need many lifetimes of death and rebirth to fulfill their desires. *This is why it is said that seekers of the Truth, Yogis, should keep their desires simple and few in number.*

Desire is the *root* Shakti. It must be watched carefully and kept in check, like one would handle a nitroglycerine stick. For every thought, word and action there is a corresponding compensation that has to be experienced in this life or the next. There is a ripple effect that occurs in every life. *The way in which the ripple comes back to you, depends on what you put out.*

For every vibration there is a corresponding reward which will either be experienced as good, bad or God, depending on your inner state. When you experience the result of your desire (and the actions taken to support it) as good, you experience pleasure. This usually begins a cycle of more actions aimed at fulfilling the same pleasurable desire. *When the source of your desire is not properly understood as God,* your desire serves to conceal your true nature from yourself. When you experience the result of your desire as being bad, the same outcome occurs, and God remains concealed. You create more and more karmas for yourself in this way.

So, if you are not living in the desireless state, every major desire you have is a potential new lifetime in the making. Karma is a huge tree with hundreds of thousands of leaves, each leaf being a lifetime that has to be experienced. This is why seekers of the Truth begin to ask a question; "How can I stop this river of desires from carrying me to endless misery?"

Now, you may feel yourself to be clever in thinking, "Well, maybe this isn't so bad. If my karmas are all good, I could just continue to come back and live life after life of pleasure." *Well, until your perceived good karmas run out. And that's if you are spiritually aware enough to ever commit only pure actions.* My Gurudev used to say karma is like making withdrawals from a bank account when you don't know what's being deposited. *You will suddenly find yourself overdrawn.* Again, remember that Karma is limiting desire and craving born of thought. The only way to begin addressing your karmic cycle to put an end to it is, first, to remember that there are no good or bad karmas, just karmas.

Back To The World of Your Inner Impressions

In the previous chapters, I have spoken about the world of your inner impressions. Understanding what karma is and how karmas are created highlights the necessity for addressing the world of your inner impressions. In spiritual life, if your goal is permanent spiritual transformation, the world of your inner impressions is the challenge to that transformation. Again, the world of your inner impressions comprises all of the impressions that have been left behind in your mind and deposited into your subtle body, of which memory is a part.

In spiritual life, an effective, daily spiritual practice is necessary to remove those impressions, while developing the ability to stop creating new ones – even while interacting in your daily, mundane existence. Such a spiritual practice must be supported by Grace and the leadership of a very good spiritual Guru. In the chapters that follow, you will be taught the first steps to permanent spiritual transformation, in order to address and improve your inner state.

Chapter 5
The Limitation of the Ego

      In Nityananda Shaktipat Yoga we refer to the ego as the ego idea. This is because the ego is borne of the notion that you are just a person, just a body with a given name, along with the mind and the senses. It is attachment to this notion that causes the ego idea to manifest.

      The limitation of the ego is a mechanism that compels you to want to manipulate and control outcomes and people, places and things. You attribute your ability to do so to your false notion of individuality – to your false notion of being just the body, mind and the senses, with a given name. The ego idea breeds both attachment and aversion to people, places and things. Attachment and aversion are one of the primary signs that your ego is engaged.

      In the early stages of life, growing up as a child and young adult, there is the question of identity and how to protect that identity. If you believe that you are just an individual with a given name and form, your tendency will always be to protect that individual identity as you go about your daily mundane activities. This is doership. You may find this to be useful. However, in spiritual life, the limitation of the ego is not useful and poses the only barrier to permanent spiritual transformation.

"Ram (another name for God) is not attained by renouncing wealth or life; Only he attains

*Narayana who renounces the pride of his
body.*

*God can never be attained by renouncing all
worldly affairs, By renouncing wife, children,
family, or household matters, By eating
only roots, tubers, and fruit, and renouncing other
foods, By renouncing clothes and going about
naked, by giving up women, Even by renouncing
one's own life force, Hari is not attained.*

*Ram is not attained by renouncing wealth or life;
Only he attains Narayana who renounces the
pride of his body.*

*By renouncing beds of flowers, diamonds, and
pearls, By renouncing one's own caste and family
traditions, By renouncing the entanglements of
this world and roaming through the forest
day and night, By renouncing remembrance of the
body and burning it to ashes, By renouncing one's
own life, without any knowledge of Brahman;*

*Ram is not attained by renouncing wealth or life;
Only he attains Narayana who renounces the
pride of his body.*

*By renouncing all speech, by observing silence and
saying nothing, By renouncing father and
grandfather and practicing yoga from childhood,
By renouncing one's own good mother, one's tuft
of hair and sacred thread, By renouncing killing
and violence and never harming any living
creature, If the pride of the body is not abandoned,
what can be attained by renouncing all these
things?*

Ram is not attained by renouncing

wealth or life; Only he attains Narayana who renounces the pride of his body.

By renouncing the bed of earth, by not sleeping but standing day and night, By renouncing all ease, doing without comforts, and undergoing hardship, By renouncing bitter words and speaking sweetly to all, By renouncing all these things but not abandoning the constant pride of the body, Banarasi says, even after renouncing all life, still He is not attained.

Ram is not attained by renouncing wealth or life; Only he attains Narayana who renounces the pride of his body." [1]
~ The Poet-Saint Banarasi

The Play of the Gunas and the Malas

In Chapter 3, I spoke of the Play of the Gunas and the Malas. You may want to review that section now. Due to the play of these impurities in the body of Supreme Consciousness, you are forced to see yourself as an object. Once you see yourself as a mere object, just a person, immediately you embrace the notion that you must become an object of someone else's desire.

This happens with intimate relating and also occurs in relationships in the workplace and elsewhere. This is due to another phenomenon that I spoke about in previous chapters. Due to the existence of individual will, the small 'I,' you come to believe that you have to become somebody in the eyes of others. And, if you don't know who you are, if you don't know from direct experience that you are the Self, you will become whoever and whatever others want you to be.

"The ego is like a black bug on a black rock on a moonless night."
~ The Poet-Saint Kabir

Per the words of Kabir above, how will you ever be able to see your ego, let alone eliminate the ego idea without an outside agent who has the microscope needed to do so? The destruction of the limitation of the ego is necessary to attain permanent spiritual transformation. This is so because until the ego idea is destroyed you will never embrace your true nature as God and you will never seek to permanently address your restless mind in order to have an ongoing, and then permanent experience that you are God – and that all others are God also. You won't be able to recognize the Play of the Shakti as this world.

There is a common fear that rises in those who here of this talk of the ego. They fear that if the limitation of the ego is destroyed, they won't have an identity. This is not so. When the destruction of the ego-idea occurs you are able to freely embrace and experience your true identity – that you are God, That, the Self. You are surrendering something so limited for something so much greater. This is the purpose of the entire spiritual journey home.

To eliminate the limitation of the ego requires the Grace, Blessings and leadership of an outside agent in a Siddha Guru. There is no other way because, just as you cannot pull yourself up in the air by your own bootstraps, you cannot eliminate the ego without the leadership of such an agent. That Guru should also be one who has been authorized to give Shaktipat by his/her own

Guru. Shaktipat is the beginning, the middle and the end. More about this in the next two chapters.

Chapter 6
The Importance of Grace for Improving Your Inner State Permanently

Grace begins with a grateful heart. The cultivated practice of giving thanks to God for the living Sadguru (true Guru), for the relationships that support you in facing all your circumstances, and for the privilege of praise and worship – this practice is the beginning of becoming fit for imbibing Grace. Therefore, in our approach, we have a saying that has become a daily offering for many: *Thank you Lord for another day to glorify you.*

God, Shiva-Shakti, your own inner essence, is pleased when you merge your individual identification with your body, mind and senses, into God. When you allow your awareness to rest in God permanently, in every thought and action, by giving God the glory, by attributing everything to the Self, by seeing God in everything and everyone everywhere, by remaining absorbed in the constant state of Blissful rapture that is the inner Self, *Grace comes looking for you and fills your life.* In this way, you please God. And pleasing God attracts even more Grace into your life.

Attaining this state frees you from all bondage, all worry, all fear, all entanglements. It frees you from ignorance forever, so that you can experience Perfect Peace, Perfect Happiness, Perfect Joy, Perfect Abundance, Perfect

Gratitude, Perfect Love, Perfect Giving and
Perfect Receiving. What's not to love about this
state?! So, why do it? You tell me! This is the part
where everyone says, "Great! Wonderful! I'm
there. I can do it!"

But there is another part that some
people get very hardheaded about. How does
one acquire this state? *This state is
not attained without the Grace and leadership of a
Siddha Guru.* Every Saint, every spiritually-
perfected Love being in our lineage says so. This
is the truth.

Make no mistake about it. If you are
seeking the inner Self, the goal is *permanent
spiritual transformation* that is had by the Grace
of a spiritual leader who lives in an
uninterrupted state of Grace. ***Even without
being Self-realized*, you can have and continue
to deepen your experiences of the Self that
can equal the state of the Self-realized beings**.
When you follow the instruction for becoming
established in these experiences, the Guru is
pleased, and God is pleased.

So, the first step is to please your Guru in
this way, by following the instruction and
obeying the Shaktipat Kriya Process (more about
this shortly) for facing yourself. This is the way
you attract the Grace necessary to experience
and realize your true nature.

Grace is all there is. My Guru used to say
that it is always raining Grace. It's just that
people put their umbrellas up and keep Grace
out. People do sabotage Grace. When it is the
Supreme Being who sees through your eyes,
hears through your ears, smells through your
nose, feels through your limbs, when this is the
case, it is Grace that rules your life. *There is
nothing but Grace.* If you don't experience it in

this way, the reason you don't experience it as such is that you have not yet aligned your will with God's Will. That is the only obstacle.

This Grace also takes the form of pure Love, Supreme Love; God's Love, the *Love without distinctions* that is experienced in the company of Saints. This Love also takes the form of the Grace-bestowing power of God that is transmitted by the Shaktipat Guru through full Kundalini Awakening, and that Guru's Kriya Shakti that engages you in Sadhana. For this reason, Bhagawan Nityananda of Ganeshpuri refers to our approach as Gurukripa Yoga, the Yoga of Guru's Grace. Lord Shiva refers to it as the *easy* means. Lord Krishna refers to it as the *only* means. *And, above all else, this Grace is God's Love, the Love of the true Heart.*

Bhakti

Bhakti means devotion. It is a reference to devotion to God and the Guru who leads the way to permanent spiritual transformation and Liberation. The foundation for Bhakti is threefold: Humility, Reverence and Longing. Bhakti cannot be cultivated without humility and reverence for God and the Guru.

This is so because God exists in our feeling. With humility and reverence our feeling for God and the desire to know God fully increases. From this increase in feeling Bhakti arises. In mundane life one cannot attain anything worthwhile without being devoted to the routine that brings the skills necessary for that attainment. In the same way, in spiritual life, nothing of lasting value can be attained without Bhakti.

Increased Bhakti gives rise to a burning longing to be free: Free of the ignorance of worldliness, free of the restless mind and free of the limitation of the ego. It is this burning longing to be free that is the 'fuel' for the necessary vigilance in daily spiritual practice that is required for permanent spiritual transformation.

Although one can begin to cultivate Bhakti by embracing God's Grace when one directs one's longing to the formless Absolute, the sages of steady wisdom of our lineage refer to this as an *inferior* means - that will only lead to glimpses of the joy, peace and love of the true heart. This is why the great beings tell us to direct our *Bhakti*, our Love and Longing *to the form* of our chosen Sadguru. This is the easiest and quickest means of attracting and imbibing the Grace-bestowing power of God.

The living Siddha Guru is the catalyst who leads you in directing your will and your longing in such a way that your Bhakti increases and increases. And it is your increased Bhakti that causes the Guru to direct his will to your receipt of more and more Grace. This Grace is God's Love and the Guru's Love.

Muralee bajat akhand sadaaye

*"The flute of the infinite is played without ceasing,
And its sound is love: When love renounces all
limits, it reaches Truth.*

*How widely the fragrance spreads! It has no end,
nothing stands in its way. The form of this melody
is bright like a million suns:*

Incomparably sounds the vina, the vina of the notes of Truth." [1]
~ The Poet Saint Kabir

As we imbibe more and more of this Grace, we come to understand and experience *living in a state of Grace.* This state of Grace is all-encompassing Love. This Love is without any distinctions, completely unconditional. It is a state of indescribable Joy!

Those who are in the habit of making distinctions in love have tainted themselves in such a way that they find the true Love of the Heart suspicious. *Ignore these suspicions.* Rise above praise and blame by the hand of this Love. Once you begin to experience the Love that living in a state of Grace delivers, you won't ever need to close your heart, even when boundaries to relating must be drawn.

A great being has said that God is bought with Love alone. If you want sublime intoxication that is so much greater than the intoxication of drugs, alcohol and sex, if you want the intoxication of inner rapture, *first become your own beloved.*

Through Love this entire Universe of all the worlds comes into being. Through Love the sun shines, the moon glows, nature sparkles, the seasons change and the clouds shed rain. This is the power of Grace. Therefore, the great beings tell us: *Make this Love without distinctions your life.* Make Love your worshipful deity and become a Love addict. Love all as your very own Self. Conquer yourself with this Love that is Grace. Then you will know for yourself what Bhakti is.

Shaktipat

What if you could experience a state of peace and indescribable joy, while calming your restless mind in less than 3 minutes, without years of meditation practice? What if you could experience unconditional love and compassion for yourself and for others while, at the same time, experiencing a state of fearlessness beyond comparison, without years of arduous struggle?

Shaktipat is the greatest spiritual initiation. After receiving it, a profound shift in my spiritual journey began very quickly. This happened within days of having this transmission of God's Grace bestowed on me. Later, I was taught about this being the first step in mastering Shaktipat Meditation and engaging what we refer to here in Nityananda Shaktipat Yoga as the *Shaktipat Kriya Process* or, simply, *Sadhana.*

I have received a number of 'initiations' in my life, some of them religious and/or spiritual (baptism as a baby, baptism in a river as a young adult, benedictions, American Indian initiation ceremonies and initiation into monastic life). But I had never experienced an initiation like this – one that was the greatest gift of my life – an initiation that spontaneously began an incredible, transforming journey of retracing my steps back to God.

Prior to receiving this blessing of Grace that also invoked healing on so many tangible levels, I had never had a personal relationship with God. I had never had the direct experience of the Absolute. My experience had been limited to intellectual knowledge with a few, short glimpses of something 'other worldly' here and there. And my spiritual attainment (or lack thereof) had never been *tested.* All of this changed under the spiritual leadership and companionship of my Shri Gurudev!

Why Shaktipat? To answer that question, here's a partial list:

- If you meditate now, you'll meditate better.
- If you don't meditate now, you'll be able to easily start a daily meditation, chanting and Mantra Yoga practice.
- You'll be set on a path to be happy for no good reason, *permanently.*
- You'll begin a process, *an unfolding* that will deliver you to lasting peace, indescribable joy, love without distinctions and the inner strength necessary to take on life's challenges with a smile on your face.
- You'll be set on a trajectory to well-being in all the areas of your life.

Most importantly, the Grace-bestowing power necessary to address and remove all the Karmic obstacles that keep you bound to fear, anxiety, doubt, worry, frustration, anger, lust, corruption due to greed, sarcasm and cynicism – this power of Grace comes by way of a Blessing that is transmitted to you. This begins a journey to an exalted state of well-being that is both incomparable and fulfilling in every way, by helping you get rid of all that you are not and releasing you from all of your karmic obstacles.

For more information about Shaktipat, visit https://www.shaktipatblessing.org/.

Chapter 7
How to Improve
Your Inner State

You may want to review the principles expressed in Chapter 2 before reading this chapter. The first step to improving your inner state is to become keenly aware of all the places that you allow your mind to roam so that you can begin to rein in the restless mind. This requires a heightened spiritual witnessing awareness that then allows you to really know your mind and the quality of your thinking from that place that is beyond the mind and beyond the senses.

In Nityananda Shaktipat Yoga, we have a very effective method for this known as Witness Consciousness Centering. This method allows you to passively observe your mind and all the places you allow it to wander into.

The challenge to your experiencing permanent spiritual transformation, and the ultimate state of Liberation that follows, is this: Invariably, you spend your time concerning yourself with comfort, security and reward before finding out who you really are. If, instead, you discovered your true nature in order to cure your amnesia, a Reality full of Grace and Blessings would unfold for you. In this way, finding your true wealth inside you will surprise you with an exemplary abundance that you already own!

For so many lifetimes you have chased after comfort, security and reward, embodied in the pursuit of pleasure, in an attempt to avoid pain. Indeed, this has resulted in the constant search for happiness where it is not. Consequently, you are always looking outside for what is not there.

My Guru used to tell the story of the musk deer. The musk deer carries the wonderful scent of musk in its own navel. And yet, when it smells that scent coming from inside itself, it follows the breeze that carries the scent into the mountains, searching for where the scent is coming from, thinking it to be somewhere outside itself.

It runs and runs after that scent, following the breeze up into the mountains. It runs and runs and eventually dies trying to find the source of that scent. Then the people living in the mountains cut open the musk deer and remove the musk! Until you find the true source of your happiness and peace, you are like that musk deer.

Happiness Is A Quiet Mind

The state of your mind determines your entire existence and the quality of that existence. A restless mind cannot produce the kind of Peace, Joy, Centeredness and Happiness that is essential for individual well-being and the collective well-being of everyone on the planet. Everyone wants to be happy. People engage in all types of behavior in search of happiness. The truth is happiness requires a mind that is free from agitation, worry, doubt, fear, anxiety and restlessness.

Inside you there is an ocean of Peace, a wellspring of Joy and Inspiration that never runs dry. To experience this, you have to go beyond your mind and beyond your senses to that

Witness to your mind and your senses. This begins by making the mind quiet so that you can experience what we call your natural, free state of being, your True nature. So, a quiet mind is essential.

What if you could experience a silent mind and then no thoughts whatsoever, followed by a wonderful experience of Peace and Joy, *in less than three minutes?* Further, what if you had a simple, daily practice in which you could maintain this experience of a silent mind, while making your mind sharper? My Shri Gurudev has said that there are many journeys in life, but that the journey to Liberation begins with the understanding *Shivo'Ham*, I am Shiva, I am the Self. This highest of understandings is imparted by the sages of steady wisdom of my lineage.

Without reaching for and embracing it in the present moment, it is impossible to stay the course long enough to face yourself. And facing yourself is done to root out the karmic obstacles to your freedom and permanent spiritual transformation. These are obstacles that you yourself have created. They prevent you from retracing your steps back to God.

"You are the one witness of everything and are always completely free. The cause of your bondage is that you see the witness as something other than this." [1]
~ Ashtavakra, from his Ashtavakra Gita

The following is an excerpt from my book *The Verses On Witness Consciousness.* [2]

1. Witness Consciousness or the State of the Observer: An experience in which you are able to watch your thoughts, emotions, notions, etc. come and go passively, without judgment and

without any reaction or response that allows the energy of egoism to arise. A state in which, from that Witness to your mind, you are able to observe that Source from which all thoughts rise, are sustained and withdrawn.

2. The purpose of practicing Witness Consciousness Centering is to begin the important process of *Remembrance* as you go about your daily, mundane activities. The great beings tell us that Remembrance means resolving one's identity crisis by identifying with the Self, with our True nature. To do so in every movement of thought, emotions, notions, etc. in our Consciousness is to experience the Witness to your mind.

3. Why do you need to be reminded? Because you forget who you really are. Through so many karmas (mental conditioning) of so many past lives and the present life, you have developed the false notion that you are just a person, a mere individual, that you are the body with an exclusive personality, that you are small, ordinary or delightfully weird. Without remembering who you really are, without being reminded constantly that you are the Self, there is no hope for permanent spiritual transformation. Finding true peace and happiness then becomes a fading dream, mostly due to the raging river of worldly distractions.

4. We know when we are thinking but how do we know we are thinking? How do we know we have slept? How do we know we have dreamt? We know because there is a higher power, a power that we refer to as *the Knower, the Witness, that Supreme Principle* that is beyond

the mind and beyond the senses. *That* is what observes these changing states of experience. That Witness is who we really are.

5. Reaching for this Witness Consciousness state, with practice and the Grace and leadership of a perfected spiritual Master, leads to your awareness merging in the experience of the Witness. In Shaivism, this merging is referred to as *Pure Perceiving Awareness.* It is a Blessing of the Grace-bestowing power that flows through a Shaktipat Guru. This Blessing also comes by way of your Grace inherent in your performance of instructed spiritual practice.

6. To begin to understand and to experience this State of the Observer known as Witnessing Awareness, it is necessary to hold and to contemplate the fundamental teaching of our approach. This is a Shakta approach (upaya) leading to the Shambava state (Liberation). It is elucidated by Shivaji in such sacred texts as the Shiva Sutras and the Spanda Karikas.

7. This instruction is framed in the utterances of the great beings of our lineage who state, "See God In Each Other. The Self Exists Equally In All."

8. In order to practice and perfect Witness Consciousness Centering, we begin by holding the highest understanding "I am Shiva. I am the Self. I am God."

9. Even if you have not yet gathered the evidence of this Truth, by way of direct experience, you can hold this understanding, this wisdom. It will help you gather the evidence of this fact by allowing you to build a foundation for going

higher. This occurs with the spiritual practice and leadership in application of this instruction that will become the proof of this Truth.

10. Without embracing the understanding "I am Shiva. I am the Self. I am God," it is impossible for us to sustain the practice of Witness Consciousness Centering long enough to shatter belief and opinion in the direct experience of the Highest. We hold this understanding, coupled with our spiritual practice as instructed by a Sadguru, to prove this statement to ourselves, in the laboratory of our own existence. Holding this understanding becomes our act of Grace.

11. Therefore, the great beings tell us "You are not a person. You are the Self. You are God."

12. In fact, your perfection is already with you. The great travesty is that you *forget* who you really are. You lose awareness of the Self, the Pure Perceiving Awareness of your own Divinity. *You lose this awareness by concealing from yourself the fact that you are the Self.*

13. The great beings tell us that the culmination of the spiritual journey rests in the experience of *never forgetting* our True nature as the Self, even when thoughts and fancies play in the mind. The point of following the instruction in the practice of this state of the Observer is *to become established in this experience of remembrance, of never forgetting.* The instruction is an act of the Sadguru's Grace.

14. Repeated here as a reminder. ☺ Perfecting the state of the Observer is a practice of *Remembrance.* We have to *practice* remembering

who we really are because, through lifetimes of useless mental conditioning (our Karmas), we are in the habit of forgetting. We forget by way of embracing the false notions that we are the body, the senses, a mere person, that we are an individual, a personality only. And we have plenty of worldly distractions that cause us to engage in this amnesia.

15. Due to these Karmas that are the foundation for our mental conditioning, we need to be constantly reminded of the Truth. "I am Shiva. I am the Self. I am God." Of course, without the Grace and daily spiritual practice that allows us to prove this in the laboratory of our own existence, we never make progress. Without Grace we can't shatter the illusion of lifetimes of the mental conditioning that keeps us bound, that keeps us believing that we are small, that we are just ordinary, that we are sinners, impure, unable to change.

16. The greatest challenge to the destruction of the Karmas that keep us entangled in what is false is how to keep our Humanity. This challenge is in how to enjoy living without remaining bound. Walking through the prison gate into the Total Freedom that comes from knowing, through direct experience, who we really are is essential.

17. This is a matter of resolving an identity crisis by inner investigation and experience – beginning with the experience of Witness Consciousness. STOP HERE FOR A MOMENT AND TAKE A DEEP BREATH. It is recommended that you use the following link to experience the practice of some centering methods that will

help you prove the import of these verses to yourself.
https://nityanandashaktipatyoga.org/dharanas. html

18. All thoughts, notions, emotions, etc. rise and fall from the same source. Everything in the world of forms is a superimposition, a projection into the body of Supreme Consciousness. Some superimpositions free us, others keep us bound. It is the nature of the Divine Conscious energy (also known as Shakti) to manifest, sustain and withdraw, thoughts/notions and emotions in our Consciousness. Therefore, it is the nature of the mind to think. This is why the great beings tell us, "Make the mind your friend by turning it within."

19. Beyond the movements in Consciousness of thoughts, emotions, etc. is the source and power which threads through these functions. When you lay hold of this power amidst the movement of thoughts, feelings and emotions in your Consciousness, you will cease to identify with these as who you are.

20. By the power of your *witnessing awareness*, you will realize that there is no difference between 'happiness' and 'sadness.' You will realize that the notions of 'happy' and 'sad' come from self-appropriating movements in Consciousness to the false notion of individuality, to the false notion that you are the body, just a person, place or thing.

21. In truth, these are the same sensations arising out of the Self, being sustained by the Self, and being withdrawn back into that very same

Self. God alone is. It is the Shiva-Shakti power alone that gives the experience. That power alone is true and worthy of our highest reverence.

22. In this way, even when your level of interacting with others must differ due to the varying roles you play, your inner experience does not shift away from that of the Witness, that Knower. In turn, this becomes the experience of your own sweet Joy, the Bliss of the Self. This is, first and foremost, an inner experience.

Shaktipat

There is no point in continuing to remain a seeker. In fact, the point of all spiritual seeking is to find a way to *end your seeking. To bring your seeking to an end, full Shakti Awakening and the leadership of a living Shaktipat Siddha Guru is necessary.* Such Beings are rare.

Just imagine starting at the top rather than the bottom. What is it like to start at the destination, rather than in search of the destination? This is the easy means of authentic Shaktipat. The point of receiving Shaktipat is to engage the means to evolve so that you come to live in a state of Grace as a constant. This is a state of rapture so profound as to leave you in awe of everything and everyone, all the time. It is a state of constant, spontaneous inspiration. It is a state of permanent, lasting inner peace filled with indescribable Joy. It is egoless.

Shaktipat, the full Kundalini awakening, is the initiation that opens the floodgates of Grace necessary to destroy all the karmic obstacles to inner Peace, Joy and the ocean of God's Love, in a way that ends your seeking. This Grace comes from a master.

Shaktipat is a spiritual awakening of awareness of your Divinity. You experience the Divine force of God within you and all around you. This Divinity is also known as God Consciousness or Supreme Consciousness. Within your being there is a dormant, spiritual awareness that is hidden. You conceal it beneath so many worldly impressions, thoughts, notions, ideas and opinions. This sleeping spiritual awareness is also known as Kundalini. Therefore, the purpose of Shaktipat Initiation is full Kundalini awakening.

After the receipt of Shaktipat you can frame your daily spiritual practice in the context of the 4 Pillars of Joy In Daily Living (see Chapter 1). That daily practice should include 60 minutes of Meditation each day, 15 minutes of chanting each day and the performance of Japa (mantra repetition) throughout each and every day. Japa is an excellent and vital method for taming the restless mind and making it quiet. This mantra repetition can be performed using the Mantra Om Namah Shivaya. You can repeat this mantra inwardly and quietly, with one repetition on inhalation and another repetition on exhalation. Alternately, you can chant along with a CD of a group chant of this mantra. You can also use a CD to chant along with to perform 15 minutes of chanting each day.

These practices work and we have documented their effectiveness over a large cross-section of people, over a period of 20 years. Remember that these practices are cumulative. The impact of them grows over time, as you remain vigilant with your practice on a daily basis. So, be patient. You may not see immediate results. But, over time you will experience the difference.

Chapter 8
The Bond of Power

You may want to review Chapter 6 before continuing with this chapter. A Shaktipat Siddha Guru is both a spiritual leader and companion on the journey to permanent spiritual transformation. Such transformation requires a bond of power that is sealed by Grace. There is the Grace of the living Guru that is the Grace-bestowing power of God inherent in the transmission of Shaktipat and the leadership in that Guru's instruction for your daily spiritual practice and the destruction of your karmas.

However, the Guru's Grace cannot have the necessary impact without your Grace. You extend your Grace by vigilantly imbibing and following the instruction of your Guru. Otherwise, there can be no bond of power.

The living Siddha Guru is not above God, but is God, just as you are God. The only difference between you and the Guru is that you have not yet attained the state that the Guru has attained. The Guru has fully blossomed, and you are still blossoming. In this regard, it is important to remember that the living Siddha Guru is the Guru-principle contained in the body of that Guru. This principle is fully active in the Guru and does not diminish, no matter how many beings that Guru transmits Shaktipat to and then leads.

This bond of power with a living Siddha Guru is an absolute necessity for permanent spiritual transformation. By company we rise and by company we fall. My Guru used to tell us that it takes only one drop of sour curd to spoil an entire vat of milk. So, it is essential to keep the best, the most useful inner and outer company as you engage in the practices to make the journey to permanent spiritual transformation.

Keeping the best inner company is a matter of keeping the company of the mantra and all the other practices designed to quiet your restless mind and turn it inward to the Self. Keeping the outer company is a matter of keeping the company of the living Guru and keeping the company of those who are headed in the same direction spiritually that you are. Naysaying is common amongst even friends and family members when they find out that you have a Guru. This is because they may feel that they will lose your love. So, you have to remind them that they will never lose your love, and that, even if they do not get involved in your chosen path, that you want their support in what you have chosen to improve yourself and your existence here.

The Guru Is The Means

There is a lot of talk of Gurus being cult leaders. People who feel this way are not to be blamed. There are many false Gurus promoting themselves online and elsewhere. These people have given their students misleading instruction and crumbs disguised as wisdom. They have never followed any Guru but want to be everyone's Guru. Beware of such people.

Because there is this 'guru market' today, people are discouraged even when hearing the word "Guru." So, it is important to understand both the necessity for a spiritual Guru and the cautions to take, because the living Guru is the means.

A Self-realized being sees only Equality in God Consciousness everywhere and in everyone. In order to lead seekers in this world of forms *in which the notions of duality and diversity have become so entrenched*, **a Sadguru also has to use that perception of duality, within the fundamental experience of Unity, in order to lead seekers to permanent spiritual transformation.** *The true Siddha Guru is free of all duality, but must use your notion of duality in order to help you strike it down, permanently.*

A true Guru also gives devotees some of what they want, so that they will want more of what the Guru has to give. This giving to devotees some of what they want and need, particularly in keeping those more in need in closer physical proximity than others, also occurs in the realm of duality that the Sadguru must use to reach people while weaning them on to longing for the Truth.

It is due to this fact that the great beings of our lineage provide us with advice on how to properly recognize and test the Guru, as you take up the instruction of such a being. *People who are invested in the false notion of individuality, of being the body and just a person can only project or superimpose this false notion on to themselves and others, because this is all they know.* Because this is the case, over a period of millennia, the holy beings of our lineage have developed a series of tests for understanding whether or not you have chosen the right one.

Medical laboratories have tests for almost every disease, virus and physical malady known to humankind. These tests have been developed, refined and perfected over a period of many, many years. So, a new lab technician does not have to come with his/her own test. He/she just has to be sure to use the test that has already been developed and proved, for the malady/deficiency, etc. that is being tested for. The tests of the Guru that are spoken of by the sages of steady wisdom of our lineage are like this.

In order to test the Guru, you will need to commit to spending some time in that beings' company, either in programs offered by the Guru or through some other form of personal contact. *The time required for this test varies dependent upon your longing for the Self.* But we're talking months, at a minimum. **Your test of the Guru should be based on your own inner experiences, the *quality* of those experiences and whether or not they deepen, over time, with your vigilance in following the instruction of that living Guru.** Do you experience a desire to know God more fully while keeping the company of the Guru and his instruction?

The primary tests spoken of by the Sadgurus of our lineage are:

1. Ours is a Shakta approach. The full Kundalini Awakening is absolutely necessary to invoke the Shaktipat Kriya Process (Sadhana or daily spiritual practice under the leadership of a Siddha Guru) that allows you to make spiritual progress *in a way that is tested*, so that you know that your progress is permanent. **There are five primary tests of a Shaktipat Sadguru.** This is the first. After receiving Shaktipat from such a being, do you have inner experiences during and/or in the weeks and months after the receipt of Shaktipat that are verifiable by the utterances of the Shaktipat Gurus of a lineage of such

beings? Did the receipt of Shaktipat catapult you into an experience of the inner Self that is worth your pursuing further?

2. The second primary test is this: Do you experience **Kriyas while in physical proximity to the Guru, while attending programs in his school or center, or while engaging in the understandings and practices the Guru has instructed you in? In other words, has your interaction with the Sadguru caused you to enter into the Shaktipat Kriya Process (Sadhana)? *If so, you know you are with a true Shaktipat Sadguru.*

3. Does the Guru have the knowledge and ability to lead you in rooting out *the Gunas and the Malas?* (see Chapter 3) Such a being should have the personal, direct experience of these being rooted out of his/her being, by the Grace and *tests* of his/her own Guru. If not, your relationship with such a being will have no lasting impact on the permanent spiritual transformation you seek.

4. In order to properly test the Guru, *you will need to follow that Guru's instruction for a daily spiritual practice, and for addressing your karmas and spiritual life,* to determine if you are having worthwhile inner experiences that are bringing you closer to the Self. *This is the fourth primary test.* You can't test the Guru without taking the Guru's medicine *for a while.* This *medicine* has

---

**Kriyas are spontaneous movements of the Shakti that occur after the receipt of Shaktipat. These Kriyas bring up latent tendencies, emotions and thoughts that make you more aware of the weaknesses that have to addressed in your Sadhana. They also make you more aware of your strengths. Kriyas are a sign that you have entered into the Shaktipat Kriya Process whereby the mirror of the Guru spontaneously reflects back to you both your strengths and weaknesses on the spiritual path.

been tested over a period of many centuries. It is *time-honored.* Just as you would not attempt to change the formula for a prescription you are given that has been proved to cure the disease you have, you should not attempt to change the instruction given by the living Sadguru for taking the medicine that will certainly cure you of your false identity.

It's only through a *vigilant* effort at following the Guru's instruction to the letter that you will be able to answer the questions "Is my mind getting quieter?" "Am I having experiences of going beyond the mind and the senses?" "Am I experiencing the thought-free state on a growing basis?" "Are the practices causing me to deepen my understanding of the inner Self while experiencing Bliss?" "Am I becoming more content?" "Is my longing for the inner Self increasing?" "Am I experiencing a growing desire to retrace my steps back to God?" Of course, if you won't take the Guru's medicine, by way of his instruction, *long enough to prove that the instruction works*, then you can't complain that the Guru is false.

5. The fifth primary test is this: Has the Guru been vested with authority and the Shakti power to initiate others, by another Shaktipat Sadguru? Does the Guru have a lineage of Self-realized beings that he/she participates in, or an acknowledged Sadguru who gave him/her the command to initiate others and lead others? And has the Guru stored up the maximum amount of Divine Conscious energy necessary to transmit God's Grace-bestowing power to others through Shaktipat and the Shaktipat Kriya Process?

In our experience, with respect to measuring the benefits of the instruction and practice taught, one should give this testing process a *minimum* of two years. For some, the growing inner experiences will provide the proof in less time. For others, it may take a little longer, if you're with the right one.

Other Necessary Tests

In Nityananda Shaktipat Yoga we encourage people to use their critical thinking in discerning whether or not the methods taught, and the leadership offered are useful and effective. In this regard we ask that students and devotees employ what we refer to as the *risk ratio test*. That test is this: Compare the experiences you have and the progress you make when following the instruction given to the letter, compare that with what happens when you don't follow the instruction. Then decide which is better for your permanent spiritual transformation.

Testing is not a 'one-way' street. If your chosen Guru is a Siddha Guru, that Guru will test your attainment and also test your willingness and resolve for permanent spiritual transformation. These tests given by the Guru happen even when you are not in close physical proximity to the Guru's form. *In Sadhana, until the final dawning of Liberation, there is where you think you are at, and then there is where you are really at.* So, the tests of the Guru as part of your Sadhana, the Shaktipat Kriya Process, is the way in which your weaknesses and strengths are always exposed.

Nityananda Shaktipat Yoga

The underlying principle that forms the foundation for all of life is *Joy*. Do you wake up with your heart singing and dancing with indescribable Joy? And are you able to sustain that Joy throughout your day? If not, why not? Our Siddha Science is a means for you to become established in a state of Grace that is pregnant with indescribable Joy!

Nityananda Shaktipat Yoga has as its foundation *Grace, Love and Light*. Here you can get rid of fear, anxiety, unhappiness and lack of well-being once and for all. *Ours is the religion of Love. The path of Supreme Love embodied in the Wisdom, Grace and Blessings of the Siddhas of our lineage.*

With this in mind, here you will experience the Siddha Science of Sages – by way of the practical leadership of Kedarji and his 4 Pillars of Joy In Daily Living. In addition, our school is run by student volunteers whose lives have been transformed by our offering.

For more information and how to begin visit www.NityanandaShaktipatYoga.org.

References

(control, shift, space bar)
Chapter 1

1. https://my.clevelandclinic.org/health/diseases/11209-weight-control-and-obesity

2. https://www.ncbi.nlm.nih.gov/search/research-news/12328/

3. https://pmc.ncbi.nlm.nih.gov/articles/PMC300778/

4. https://www.cdc.gov/obesity/childhood-obesity-facts/childhood-obesity-facts.html

https://stateofchildhoodobesity.org/demographic-data/ages-6-17/

https://www.cdc.gov/diabetes/php/data-research/index.html

7. https://www.heart.org/-/media/PHD-Files-2/Science-News/2/2024-Heart-and-Stroke-Stat-Update/2024-Statistics-At-A-Glance-final_2024.pdf

8. https://www.cdc.gov/cancer/data/index.html

9. https://www.statista.com/statistics/280700/new-cancer-cases-and-deaths-in-the-us-by-gender/

10-11. DPL, pgs. 19-48 + FINAL REPORT: COVID Select Concludes 2-Year Investigation, Issues 500+ Page Final Report on Lessons Learned and the Path Forward - https://oversight.house.gov/release/final-report-covid-select-concludes-2-year-investigation-issues-500-page-final-report-on-lessons-learned-and-the-path-forward/

12. DPL pgs. 40-41, 46, 49 https://oversight.house.gov/release/final-report-covid-select-concludes-2-year-investigation-issues-500-page-final-report-on-lessons-learned-and-the-path-forward/

Chapter 2

1. Pg. 25, Shiva Sutras, Motilal Banarsidaas Publishers, Delhi, India, ISBN 978-81-208-0407-4.

2. Sutra 5, Pg. 59, Pratyabhijnahrdayam, Motilal Banarsidaas Publishers, Delhi, India, ISBN 81-208-0323-x.

3. The Concise Yoga Vashishtha, Swami Venkateshananda, State University of New York Press, Albany N.Y., ISBN 0-87395-954-X PB.

Chapter 4

1. Pgs. 29, 75, 76, The Sutras On The 5-Fold Act of Divine Consciousness, The Bhakta School of Transformation, Inc. Boardman, Ohio, ISBN 979-8-218-19915-9

Chapter 6

1. Verse 126, pg. 96, Songs of Kabir by the Poet
Saint Kabir, translated by Rabindranath Tagore,
Martino Fine Books, Mansfield Centre, CT ISBN:
978-1614277620

Chapter 7

1. Verse 1.7, pg. 15, Ashtavakra Gita by
Ashtavakra, translated by, Rajiv Kapur,
http://www.rajivkapur.com

2. Pgs. 11-16, The Verses On Witness
Consciousness, The Bhakta School of
Transformation, Boardman, Ohio, ISBN: 978-0-
578-38070-4

About Kedarji

"Love is all there is. Grace is God's Love. The awakening into Pure Perceiving Awareness, Infinite Awareness of the Highest that we refer to as Shaktipat is Love. The journey to recognition of our true nature is Love. Ours is an approach where we lead with Love. In the end, it all comes back to Love." ~ Kedarji

Wisdom and Joy! If you had leadership that can deliver you to being happy for no good reason, becoming immersed in a state of Joy and inner Peace – leadership that results in your experience of everlasting Joy in every area of your life, why not embrace it?

Bhakta School Founder

Kedarji is the Founder of The Bhakta School of Transformation. The Bhakta School is an Ohio-based not-for-profit public charity devoted to lasting Inner Peace and permanent spiritual transformation. The curriculum offering here is based on Kedaji's 4 Pillars of Joy In Daily Living

He had an early career in the Performing Arts as an actor and singer in Broadway musicals, plays, movies and television. He went on to study violin and conducting at the Juilliard School of Music. Then he graduated with degrees in performance and composition from the Manhattan School of Music. Later, he studied Eastern and Oriental Medicine. He graduated with degrees in both from the Kushi Institute and had a practice in New York City for many years.

Leading With Love

Kedarji helps people embrace the Grace in life's joys and challenges in a way that causes lasting happiness and peace. In a world seemingly mad with greed and corruption, Kedarji has a long track record of helping people affirm and expand the best parts of their lives.

He is a Siddha in the lineage of the great sage and saint, Bhagawan Nityananda of Ganeshpuri. He imparts the same instruction and leadership he was taught. These are the same methods used by a line of spiritually proven and powerful masters who have uplifted people's lives for thousands of years.

A Siddha is one who has made the commitment to live as an ascetic. Such a being renounces the pursuit of worldly pleasures and fantasies to serve the greater good and to work to uplift humanity. In this regard, Kedarji is known as a true spiritual leader. He is also known as a Shaktipat Guru (see below) *who leads by example* in becoming both wise and well *with a powerful, heart-centered approach.*

Practical Leadership In A Shaktipat Guru

Kedarji has a reputation for leading without insisting that people follow. This allows students and seekers to come to our approach in their own way. Kedarji is in a lineage of Sadgurus on whose shoulders he stands and takes refuge in. This is the great Shiva lineage that Bhagawan Nityananda of Ganeshpuri also made, of which Kedarji is a part.

Wise, Happy and Well

Many of Kedarji's students say that, through his leadership, he has transformed their lives in profound ways. And in ways they have not experienced in other modalities or on other paths.

His students blossom and uncover hidden strengths through a well-integrated and time-tested approach. Through his leadership, it's possible for anyone and everyone to *experience life's magic.* And this is experienced in a way that they come to know their true nature and attain a state of lasting happiness, peace and joy.

His 4 Pillars of Joy In Daily Living are *the Spiritual Power, Improved Mental State, Emotional Resilience and Vibrant Health.* These form the foundation that he combines the power of Grace of his spiritual lineage. This is the time-honored Siddha Science of the Yoga of the Siddhas. This powerful combination includes his skill as a Shaktipat Meditation master and his many years of practice as a practitioner of Eastern and Oriental medicine.

Authentic Shaktipat Guru – Shaktipat Meditation Master

Kedarji is a Shaktipat Guru. He has been vested with the power and authority to fully awaken and nurture the dormant spiritual awareness known as Kundalini. Specifically, this awakening occurs by way of the transmission of the Grace-bestowing power inherent in the Blessing of Shaktipat. In particular, you will find that Kedarji is a recognized and very skilled spiritual leader and Shaktipat Meditation Master. Additionally, he has the ability to lead you on the journey to the realization of your true nature. Indeed, this is a journey in which you retrace your steps back to God.

Author/Producer

Kedarji is the author of several books and courses, including:

- *Vibration of Divine Consciousness. A Spiritual Autobiography.*
- *The Verses On Witness Consciousness.*
- *The Abode of Grace – Bhagawan Nityananda of Ganeshpuri.*
- *Contemplations On the Amritanubhava of Shri Jnaneshwar Maharaj.*
- *How To Be Fearless, Happy and Resilient In The Age of Noise and Distractions.* (a video home-study course and weekend retreat).
- *The Sutras On The 5-Fold Act of Divine Consciousness.*
- *Live Strong and Be Happy. Learn The Daily Rituals of The Most Spiritually-Powerful, Happiest and Healthiest People On The Planet.*
- *Dharma and the Preservation of Liberty. The Globalist Threat to Our Freedom And What to Do About It.*
- *The Courage To Love*
- *Your Inner State Is Your Fate*

Spiritual Journey

Kedarji began his quest to understand and fully imbibe Yoga Science at an early age. Feeling incomplete, he began an intense spiritual journey that took him to India and Asia. Soon after, he experienced an initiation, an awakening into the power of true Meditation, Chanting and Contemplation. This formed the foundation for putting all the pieces together.

Due to this event and ongoing application of the methods taught connected to it, Kedarji was able to fully apply the science behind well-being that is based on the Spiritual Power. He calls it the energy substratum of everything. His direct, unfolding experience of this power is the basis for the integration of his 4 Pillars of Joy In Daily Living. This is an approach that combines Siddha Science and the science of a holistic lifestyle of health and well-being with the transmission of Grace that he extends as a God-realized, Shaktipat Guru.

Come Join Us

You can find out who Kedarji is by spending some time in the company of this Shaktipat Guru. Moreover, this is also the best way for you to experience how the power of Grace and Siddha Science skills mastery that he transmits can impact your life for the better.

Come join us to be with Kedarji and our spiritual & well-being community. Doing so, you will experience the profound leadership that awaits you here. You will find Kedarji to be an outgoing, warm and accessible leader with a great sense of humor. Equally welcoming and skilled is our staff of teachers. We hope to welcome you soon to our programs.

Board of Directors
The Bhakta School of Transformation

www.ingramcontent.com/pod-product-compliance
Lightning Source LLC
Chambersburg PA
CBHW061654120626
46550CB00003B/941